THE OTHER SIDE OF THE STREET

For Noel Lloyd and Geoffrey Palmer, who encouraged me to dig into my memories and helped me to turn chaos into order.

JEAN ALEXANDER

THE OTHER SIDE OF THE STREET

THE AUTOBIOGRAPHY OF
JEAN ALEXANDER

Lennard Publishing
1989

Lennard Publishing
a division of Lennard Books Ltd
Musterlin House
Jordan Hill Road
Oxford OX2 8DP

British Library Cataloguing in Publication Data
is available for this title.

ISBN: 1 85291 064 X

First published 1989
© Hermitage Books 1989

Phototypeset in Bembo (Linotron 202)
by Goodfellow & Egan, Cambridge
Designed by Geoff Green
Cover design by Pocknell & Co.
Reproduced, printed and bound in Great Britain by
Butler and Tanner Limited, Frome and London

CONTENTS

LIST OF ILLUSTRATIONS

Mother and dad's engagement photographs (1917)
Grandpa Hill (1915)
Ken (aged 3½) and me (aged 1½)
Ken (aged 5) and me (aged 3)
Ken and me (aged 4) in hand-me-down jersey, Barrow Park
Grandma Hill, mother and me (aged 8)
Me (aged 9)
Just after leaving the library service, when I was 23 years old
With The Adelphi Guild Theatre at Macclesfield (1951)
My first professional appearance (1949)
With Noel Lloyd in *The Prince of Darkness is a Gentleman*, Macclesfield (1951)
Programme for *Uncle Harry*, Scala Theatre, Southport
As Marty in *Anna Christie*, Theatre Royal, York
Programme for *A View From the Bridge*, York
With Bunny at our special anniversary party to celebrate 10 years on The Street (1974)
With Bernard Youens and Sheila Price in *Arsenic and Old Lace* at Oldham (1975)
With my mother and brother Ken (1978)
In my role as mascot for a Welsh Rugby team
Hilda with *Coronation Street's* Bobby
Being presented to the Queen, Palace Theatre, Manchester (1977)
With Sir John Betjeman
A studio portrait (1982)
In my conservatory (1983)
With my R.T.S. Award (1985)
At home in Southport
Hilda with *Our Hilda* rose (1986)
My leaving party with the cast of *Coronation Street* (1987)

Before . . .

MANY people have asked me, 'What did you do before you became Hilda Ogden?' or even, 'Who were you before you were Hilda Ogden?'

The answers are in this book . . .

I have delved into my memory, my scrapbooks and photograph albums, and I have tried to re-discover the little girl who lived in a poor part of Liverpool, had loving parents and brother, and a secret ambition to be an actress. I have followed her through her war years, her first job in a library, her adventures as a fanatical theatre-goer, her eventual entry into the world of the professional theatre and her early struggles and disappointments until *Coronation Street* brought her fame and security.

Coronation Street took up more than a third of my life and two-thirds of my acting career; but there was a Jean Alexander before I stepped into the Granada studios, and there has been a Jean Alexander since I left the programme; and here she is in these pages.

I view Hilda Ogden with mixed feelings. I enjoyed working in *The Street* and it was a joy to have Bernard Youens as a partner. Granada was a marvellous and generous company to work for and over the years I made many friends among the cast. It was by far the best job I ever had and I am grateful to the millions of people who enjoyed Hilda's antics twice a week. I respected the character of Hilda, who grew to be much more than the slattern she was originally meant to be. She was a spunky little soul, a fighter, like one of those lead-bottomed dolls that returns to upright when it is knocked down.

Yes, she was good to me and there was a lot in her that I admired, but she ceased to exist the moment I took out my curlers, folded my pinny, re-arranged my hair and stepped into the real world at the end of each recording. There was no nonsense about the character taking me over. I would have hated it if Hilda had lived in my house! Now she is part of my past, and I am experiencing a new career which is full of interest and challenges.

I entered the theatre by a lucky chance and luck has been with me throughout. That, together with determination, hard work and a sense of humour, saw me through years of slavery in repertory companies, and helped me through times when work was thin and pavements hard. And always there were my family and friends to console and encourage me and make me laugh. I have been, and am, a very fortunate person, and I have not come to the end of things, not by a long chalk!

CHAPTER 1

Rhiwlas Street

MY BROTHER Ken had perfect pitch, even at the age of three. One evening during a variety show at the Pivvy (the Pavilion Theatre in Lodge Lane, Liverpool) he became infuriated by the off-key singing of a large soprano. Suddenly, anguish written on his face, he clambered on to his seat, pointed a stubby little finger at the stage and piped shrilly, 'Off! Off! Off!' and the sound reverberated round the whole theatre.

I was one year old and asleep throughout the performance, so I could not join the family embarrassment. I am told that the singer was visibly shaken but managed to finish her number. Back at home Ken, after a verbal chastisement, could not understand what he had done wrong. 'She was singing all funny,' he insisted.

Ken became Head of the Classics Department at Altrincham Grammar School in Cheshire, and also a very talented pianist, composer and arranger. I eventually donned pinny and curlers and changed into Hilda Ogden of *Coronation Street* with my own rendering of *Amapola* giving new meaning to the verb 'to render'. My musical ability in real life is about on a par with Hilda's, though, unlike her, I am passionate about classical music, particularly Beethoven. When I was a child singing, as I thought, like Melba, Ken would shake me and cry, 'Mum, stop her, stop her, it's awful!'

I was born in Liverpool in 1926. That should have a sort of resonance about it because Liverpool has, over the years, become famous for many things, culminating, perhaps, in the Beatlemania of the 1960s and after. But Liverpudlians were proud of their city many years before the four lads embarked on their phenomenal careers. As children we took for granted that it was the best place in the world. It had miles of thriving docks and a couple of illustrious football teams. The darkly Grecian St George's Hall, massive and dignified, stood, as the witticism said, 'behind the Punch and Judy Show'. The twin-pinnacled Liver Building, surmounted by its Liver Birds, welcomed new arrivals to the port. There were friendly ferry boats chugging to and from the Wirral seaside towns, little boats that had bravely gone over to the Continent in the First World War and were to do a similar job in the Second.

Other cities had their attractions, we were first to admit, but they could not hold a candle to ours. We had a neo-Gothic cathedral beginning to dominate the city from St James' Hill, and we had wonderful theatres – the Empire, the Royal Court, the Playhouse, the Pavilion and, though not quite as respectable, the Rotunda. All the great names in variety and the straight theatre came to play in them, and the Philharmonic Hall took a lot of beating for those who liked 'proper' music.

Rhiwlas Street, in the Toxteth area, was my birthplace. I was born two years after Ken, and we were the only children, quite content to play together, to fight and make up, and become allies against the grown-ups. My father Archie was an electrician, and we lived with him and Nell, my mother, in a small terraced house.

Today Toxteth is synonymous with riots, fires, grisly rundown estates and racial tension. In the uncertain world of the 1920s and 1930s it was a poor area, but poverty is often a relative term and we were never aware of deprivation. The people of Toxteth lived bravely, scrubbed their front doorsteps every morning and were always ready to help friends and neighbours in trouble. That spirit of defiance against the malign forces that seek to pull people down is still in evidence. Rhiwlas Street still exists and continues to epitomise the determination, humour and resilience of Liverpool people.

No. 18 was similar in many ways to the houses in *Coronation Street* which are based on reality, but it was more primitive. It had three bedrooms, no bathroom, and a horrendous outside loo. I call it 'horrendous' because it was no fun making a trip to the back yard on a cold winter's night. In all other respects it was all a lavatory should be:

my lovely, respectable down-to-earth mother saw to that. In the house the furniture was on the sparse side, and most things had been bought second-hand, but they were dusted and polished as though they were priceless antiques.

My father worked for a firm of electrical engineers which specialised in shipyard contracts, so he was away from home a lot, sometimes for a month at a time, either at Southampton, Belfast, Barrow or Glasgow. His wages during my early years were not more than £3 a week and he was not paid for holidays. We missed him very much when he was away and his return was always a joyous occasion, not least because there was always some small present for Ken and me. He was not a very demonstrative person. His words were few but carefully chosen and exactly right for the occasion, and because of his direct and uncomplicated nature he got on with everybody. He was very self-contained, never got into a flap, and if he said, 'That's it!' that *was* it. His word was law, and our love for him was tinged with a little awe; there was always a slight distance between him and his children. But what was so good was the feeling of stability, and the knowledge that when he was around the world would never go wrong.

Because dad was away so much the bringing up of Ken and me devolved on our mother. She moulded and directed us, gave us loving hugs and sometimes slaps that hurt. It was she we argued with, cajoled and ran to in times of childish crisis. And if we misbehaved she had only to say, 'I'll tell your father' and all wickedness would stop. We knew that he would never lay a finger on us but we did not want him to know that we had been naughty.

As far as we were concerned, dad never did anything wrong. He was the upright one, the head of the family; he brought home the money and kept us all going. In my funny girlish way I always tried to be like him, to emulate his quietness and reserve and live up to his standards; and I feel in many ways I have grown up with a lot of his characteristics. He was very fair-minded and I hope I am too. He could see both sides of a question – though I go further and sit uncomfortably on the fence because I can't make up my mind which side I'm on. I count myself fortunate in having had such caring, loving parents in times that were often hard and lacking in material comforts. They

3

taught us how to be independent and determined, to despise hypocrisy, and to keep our feet on the ground whatever our heads were doing in the clouds. When the time came for Ken and me to return that care and love and make their old age as happy and comfortable as possible it was a joy and a privilege to be able to do so.

Just after my fourth birthday I started at a primary school called Upper Park Street School which was only a few streets away from home. There was one busy main road to cross – Northumberland Street – so mother always took Ken and me to school in the morning and met us at the corner of the street in the afternoon. One day she was a little late but I saw her on the opposite side of the road, waiting for a chance to cross. 'Mum!' I called and, in my eagerness to reach her, stepped off the pavement, right into the path of a huge lorry that was thundering down on me. If it had not been for Ken's presence of mind I would have been annihilated. But he grabbed me and flung me back on the pavement with such force that I landed on my backside and sustained a severe bruise. I began to howl and mother knew that at least I was alive. She stood helpless as the lorry went by, not being able to see what was happening. 'It was the worst moment of my life,' she would say dramatically when recounting the story. My howls continued all the way home, compounded partly of fright, partly of fury at having been so unceremoniously treated, but chiefly of pain. Life is full of hazards for the unwary . . .

In the months before I started school I acquired a phobia, a feeling of great insecurity. It was as though there was a demon of some kind lurking round every corner or behind each door ready to pounce, and I was unable to let my mother out of my sight. I trailed after her all day long, following her so relentlessly that her patience became almost exhausted. When she went shopping or took Ken to school I was there, a determined little incubus clinging to her skirt. Problems arose, however, when the weather was too wet, cold or foggy for me to accompany her. On one very rainy day she refused point blank to take me with her. I stood on the doorstep and yelled my head off.

'All right then,' she said, fearful of being accused of infanticide, or at least child cruelty, 'you can come but you'll have to wear this mackintosh cape of Ken's. It's too big for you but there's nothing else.' This was the time when I was beginning to realise that most of the everyday clothes I wore had once belonged to my brother, and resentment was growing, though I could not have explained my reluctance to face the world half boy and half girl. So I refused the offer of the cape and started to scream again. Mother rarely lost her temper completely with me, though she sometimes pretended to, but on this occasion I had driven her tolerance over the edge. She dragged me into the kitchen, stood me on a little stool at the sink, put my head under the cold water tap and turned it on fully.

The shock of the cold water beating on my head was so great that I stopped screaming and started to drown – at least, that's what it seemed like at the time. I suppose my head was only under the tap for a few seconds then I was hastily removed and a towel wrapped round me, but the memory of that incident led to frequent childish nightmares and I developed a fear of water that has never quite left me. For years I would retreat from advancing waves, even having a bath was fraught with the dread of slipping below the water level and gurgling my way to oblivion.

My confidence was not increased by another incident that happened a couple of years later, at primary school. Once a week we were taken to Lodge Lane Swimming Baths for swimming lessons, and I was getting on quite nicely. I couldn't exactly swim but I could stand in the shallow end and almost swim one stroke, gradually getting up confidence to extend my range. There were changing cubicles along the side of the pool and one day I was given one near the deep end. I got into my costume and prepared to join my friends at the shallow end when a horrid little boy came dashing up, running by the pool's edge. When he got level with me, instead of swerving to the side to avoid me, he gave me a push that landed me in six feet of water. I couldn't swim and nobody had noticed ... Of course I went right under, came up again, gasping and spluttering, and sank again. I had heard that sinking for the third time means that you never come up again, and so I was determined that twice was enough for me. To this day I do not know how I did it, but I managed to dog paddle to the edge of the pool where I clung on to the bar, exhausted and terrified.

I did not learn to swim until I was fourteen and made up my mind to overcome my fears. A friend and I went to the local swimming baths, I having said loudly that I would stay in the water until I could swim. It took me two hours before I achieved a curious mixture of breast stroke and dog paddle, but I went home triumphant – I could stay in the water with my feet off the bottom!

Even now I am not very proficient and cannot bear to put my face under water. I will only swim in a pool, not in the sea, and if there is any horseplay near me I get out immediately. Only once have I swum in the sea and that was in the Caribbean. I would walk out till my head stuck out of the water and swim back to the shore using my own special stroke. When I found myself swimming for dear life in six inches of water, my knees hitting the sand, then I got up. If my head gets covered I can still see the white sink and feel the drenching force of the water and the pounding in my ears. I have come to the conclusion that the best use for water is for cruising on.

All this because I refused to wear that mackintosh cape! When I told my mother, years later, how much I had hated wearing Ken's old clothes she said, 'Nonsense, you didn't really mind,' then added doubtfully, 'Did you?'

Then I told her the story of the jersey. Ken used to wear a jersey with a little collar and long tie attached – as all little boys did in those days. It was washed so often and shrank so much that by the time it came to me there was only a mere two inches of tie sticking out under my chin and almost choking me. Ken would then flaunt himself in his new jersey with a tie almost long enough to trip over.

'I can't remember that,' my mother said.

'Well, I can,' I replied, 'and I'll find a photograph to prove it.' So I dug into my box of bits and pieces and found a tiny snap of Ken and me sitting on a railing in the park. He was in a new jersey with a flowing tie and I in his cast-off with the stubby tie under my chin. My mother was forced to admit that the wearing of handed-down clothes had taken place. 'We just could not afford new clothes for you both. You needed them at the same time, so it seemed only right for the elder to have first go. But I didn't realise at the time how deeply you felt about it.'

Christmas was a great occasion for Ken and me. We did not get many toys during the year so we looked forward with great excitement to opening our stockings on Christmas morning. Not that there was anything very expensive or unusual to be found there – a jigsaw puzzle, perhaps, a pair of socks or a box of handkerchiefs, a Dinkie toy for Ken, a doll's teaset for me, an apple, an orange and always a sugar pig on top of everything else. We would wake up about five o'clock, when it was still dark, and for a little while stay in bed, savouring the moment to come. Ken had a great fear of the dark, which he would never admit to, and relying on his seniority he would always make me get out of bed and fumble about, feet on the cold linoleum, until I had found the light switch. Then the bold lad would say, 'As you're already out of bed you can get the stockings and we'll look at our presents.'

One year, however, the worm turned and I said, 'No!' firmly. So Ken had to conquer his fear and stumble out of bed first. When we had emptied the contents of the stockings on to the counterpane and had compared presents – we each wondered why the other had got the best toy – Ken, well known for his sweet tooth, would gobble up his sugar pig in a minimum number of bites, then cast a longing look at mine. But knowing that it would be a long time before such a delicacy came my way again, I would put it under the pillow and save it for a special occasion when I could be on my own and savour every mouthful. It usually lasted till Easter and by then it was grey and grubby and I threw it away unfinished.

We were a very close family. When my father was at home we went out together or stayed at home together. Ken and I never went short of any of the necessities of life, even though luxuries were few and far between. When I was old enough to notice I realised that my mother never had a new coat. She had one dress for best and the rest of the time she wore something to work in – blouse and skirt, and an apron. She never used make-up but she always looked fresh and well-groomed, and a casual observer would never guess how poor we really were. The care and love we children received were worth more than all the smart clothes and expensive toys we sometimes longed for, and I think we knew that, without being able to express our feelings. I am sure that is why I have never lusted after cars or grand houses. St Laurent and Gucci are as distant from me now as they were fifty years ago, and the shops in Bond Street are for window-shopping and not for spending money in.

It was an exciting time when we went to Barrow-in-Furness for a couple of months to be with my father, who was, as usual, working on a ship. We stayed with his landlady, a Mrs Allington, a stout lady with suspiciously black hair, who had been on the halls when she was young and now took in variety performers appearing for a week at His Majesty's Theatre. She was, I realise now, the theatrical landlady *par excellence*. While we were there a troupe of dancing girls, about 12 of them, I think, shared the top attic rooms and practised their routines in the back yard. I thought they were wonderful and would watch them for hours. When I was alone I would try to copy their intricate steps, but it never seemed to work for me and I soon gave up all thoughts of joining the troupe. But some of the glamour which covered them like stardust worked its way into my young heart and stayed there, hidden like a seed that is going to flower in some distant spring.

Mrs Allington would swear like a trooper – out of every five words three would be 'bloody'. But she made us feel very welcome, took Ken and me under her wing and fed us sumptuously. She kept a cigarette machine in the hall for the benefit of her lodgers. It disgorged ten Woodbines for twopence, and I felt very privileged to be allowed to put the two pennies in when Mrs Allington needed a smoke. Unfortunately for the lodgers she smoked so heavily that the machine was nearly always empty.

There was a pocket handkerchief garden in front of the house and Ken and I were allowed to play on the path. One day our harmless game of football was interrupted by the lady next door who told us we were being too noisy and ordered us indoors. We crept in, crestfallen, to be met in the hall by our landlady. 'I told you bloody kids to bloody well play outside – what have you bloody come in for?'

'The lady next door told us not to play-' Ken began timidly.

'What!' Mrs Allington's bosom swelled with rage. She swept out and confronted her neighbour. 'Don't you bloody well tell my bloody kids what to bloody well do. I sent them to play in the bloody garden and that's where they'll bloody well play!'

But we didn't. We retreated to the back garden and watched the dancing girls instead. Later Ken said to mother, 'Mum, doesn't Mrs Allington talk funny?'

'Yes, but you're not to talk funny like her,' my mother replied.

That summer in Barrow was a golden time. I remember the sun, the lazy days on the beach with bucket and spade, ice cream cornets, and chips, smothered in salt and drenched in vinegar, that we ate out of a newspaper. Walney Island was just across the water from Barrow, reached by a causeway with a toll bridge at the Barrow end, and it cost a penny to go over to the island by tram. To us children it was like venturing into the unknown Congo. Although we used the tram nearly every day at home in Liverpool this one over the toll bridge had a mysterious quality about it that thrilled us every time we clambered aboard.

Near our boarding house there was a park with a theatre – or rather a marquee with a primitive stage at one end. Mum and dad would sometimes take us there in the early evening. I don't remember much of what happened there, or what kind of acts would be of such poor quality that they had been reduced to performing in a tent in a park, but one act does stand out in my memory. It was the first, but not the last time I considered that I had been defrauded in the theatre and not given value for money.

The act was an illusionist, billed as the Great Something-or-other, direct from his triumphs at Wherever-it-was. 'Ladies and gentlemen,' he boomed to his sparse audience, 'I am going to show you the world's greatest illusion.' I sat, trembling with anticipation, not quite sure what an illusion was but convinced that something magical was about to happen. 'I am going to put a man in a box, nail him down so that he cannot get out, by whatever means he tries, then hey presto! I shall use my great powers to make him re-appear in one minute before your very eyes!'

Wonderful, I thought, I am going to watch the impossible! Another man climbed into what looked like a huge packing-case on its side, and the magician hammered nails into the lid with exaggerated flourishes. Then, wiping imaginary perspiration from his brow, he invited a member of the audience to agree that the lid was firmly closed and that the man inside could not get out. A curtain was then drawn across the front of the case and with more flourishes the magician disappeared behind it. We sat on our hard seats, me chewing my handkerchief with impatience. From behind the curtain we could hear the sound of banging, heavy breathing and some low-keyed oaths. After what seemed like a lifetime the curtain was pulled aside and out of the lidless box stepped the magician's assistant, tousled and bewildered.

The magician himself bowed low, inviting our applause. He didn't get any from me. Even at that age I didn't think it was much of a trick.

A lot of things seemed to happen to me when I was round about four years of age, but the best thing of all was my actual fourth birthday. Dad, as usual, was working away from home but he managed to send some money for me to buy my own present. I believe it was seven shillings and sixpence, an unprecedented amount of money for a present. He must have been working overtime because it was almost a quarter of his normal weekly wage. I danced by my mother's side all the way from the tram stop to Blackler's, the department store in Great Charlotte Street. Ken and I climbed the marble staircase, which in my eyes was straight out of a king's palace, to the Toy Department. In front of the counter was a three-tier stand filled with a pyramid of teddy bears of all shapes, sizes and colours. Those at the bottom were small, brown and cuddly. Those halfway up were bigger, not quite so good, and right at the top in single splendour was a huge bear. I lost my heart to it immediately. 'How much is that one at the top?' I asked.

'They are all seven and sixpence,' mum said.

'I want that one,' I said, pointing.

'But, Jean, one of the little ones would last much longer. That big one will come to pieces before you can say Jack Robinson.'

I stuck out my lower lip and looked obstinate. I had no intention of saying Jack Robinson! Mother recognised my unyielding expression and hastily gave in.

'All right, you can have the big one, but I warn you . . .'

So the big bear was taken down and put on the floor next to me. It was just as tall as I was. Quality or no quality, this bear, I knew, was going to be my friend for life. I clutched it fiercely, declined to have it wrapped up, and we returned to the stop and caught a tram for home.

Trams had long wooden slatted seats facing each other down the length of the car. Mother, laden with shopping, sat down, Ken next to her. The bear was too big to be accommodated on my lap so it had to have a seat to itself, next to me. There were some interested looks from people sitting opposite but the journey started without incident. It was not long before Ken piped up. 'Mum, is it a he-bear or a she-bear?'

'Sh,' said my embarrassed mother, trying to avoid the eyes of the other passengers and pretending not to hear a snigger.

'But, mum, is it?'

'Be quiet. Anyway, why do you want to know?'

'If we don't know Jean won't know what to call it.'

Nobody could fault that logic, and mother whispered, 'I suppose it's a boy bear . . .'

Ambrose still sits in my bedroom, very battered, but conscious that he is the most important person in the house.

Ken had a teddy bear long before Ambrose appeared on the scene, but his bear had not been bought locally. My father, working in Belfast, had sent it from a small Post Office near the shipyard. As the clerk put the strangely-shaped parcel on the scales it made a sound like an angry sheep. Talking bears were not all that common in Belfast and the startled man jumped back. 'What's that?'

'Just a bear,' said my father casually.

'You're sure it's not a bomb?'

'Now why would I be sending a bomb to my son for his birthday?' said my father.

The clerk thought for a moment. 'True,' he said, 'that wouldn't be likely, would it?' and he accepted the parcel without further demur.

Ken kept Bruin until the time he was due to leave for Cambridge. By that time the animal was a sorry ruin rather than a Bruin, eyeless, legless and armless. The last thing Ken did before going to catch his train was to wrap him up carefully and, after a tender farewell, deposit him in the dustbin.

I caught pneumonia when I was four – that fateful year in my life. It was nearly my last year too for I was very ill. I was in bed for several weeks and was just starting to convalesce when I had one of the most terrifying experiences of my life. It was on Good Friday, the day when Liverpool people used to 'burn Judas' – a custom I have never heard being observed anywhere else, and I don't know if it is still carried on in Liverpool. People, young ones usually, went round the streets with an effigy of Judas on a pole, to commemorate the disciple's betrayal of Jesus before the first Easter Sunday. Householders would give them a few coppers towards their bonfires, on which the effigy would eventually be burned.

To attract the attention of people who might still be in bed the pole would be rattled against the first floor windows – and I awoke to hear a scrabbling noise and then saw a horrible ghastly face leering at me from outside. I saw the glaring eyes and lolling tongue, and I screamed. Downstairs mother thought I had had a sudden relapse and was dying noisily and she flew upstairs – to find me, white-faced, sitting up in bed and pointing at nothing, for the face had disappeared.

'You've had a nightmare,' my mother said accusingly, but she believed me when she looked out of the window and saw the procession moving down the street, and she cuddled me back to calmness. I still get a frisson of terror whenever I remember 'burning Judas'.

CHAPTER 2

Living with Grandpa

SOME TIME before my illness we had moved from Rhiwlas Street to my mother's parents' house in Arnold Street, not far away, to have more space for two growing children. The new house was much grander; it had three storeys and cellars, and we rented rooms on the first floor for fifteen shillings a week. Ken and I found it very different from our old home. We were really only used to having one other person around, and here were not only grandpa and grandma but also three of their sons, my uncles Bill, Harold and Walter. It seemed positively crowded.

Grandpa Hill's first name was Isaac and grandma's was Sarah, though grandpa called her Nellie, as her second name was Ellen. There was nothing Biblical about either of them except that grandpa's temper resembled that of an Old Testament prophet who had discovered his tribe worshipping a golden calf. His rages were phenomenal and could be conjured up in seconds. He came to dominate my life for many years in that his presence in the house was more overbearing than that of all the other members of the family put together. In appearance, when he was reasonably good-tempered, there was little outstanding about him. In fact, he was rather insignificant, of middle height, balding but, as though in compensation, he had grown a large moustache; and he had a sallow complexion. But when his temper flared up the skin round his nose turned white, his eyes glared redly like a lion's, and he seemed to grow two feet in height. Then he would utter in a terrible voice his favourite oath, 'GREAT JUMPING JESUS CHRIST!' and it was time for Ken and me to flee. Sarah took his rages in her stride, but his sons when young had been thoroughly cowed and often talked of the beatings they had received, usually for very minor breaches of conduct. Only my mother stood up to him, and when she did, scornful and defiant, he would collapse like a punctured balloon.

Grandpa had run away to sea when he was 15 and had rounded Cape Horn in a sailing ship, but after two years he ran back home and became a shunter on the railway. He had been retired for many years and every month would go over to Edge Hill Station (the Clapham Junction of Liverpool) to collect his railway pension of five shillings a week. He once asked Ken if he would like to accompany him to the railway office. Ken, who was mad about trains, jumped up and down with excitement and impatience until they were ready to start off, but when they returned two hours later his face was down to his boot tops.

'What's the matter with you?' mother asked. 'Lost a shilling and found sixpence?'

Ken sniffed miserably. 'I thought we were going to see all the engines in the shunting yard.'

'Well, didn't you?' mum said.

'No, we didn't,' Ken replied with a louder sniff. 'We were in the office for about five minutes, then we went straight to the cemetery.'

Mum stopped her dusting. 'The cemetery?'

'Yes, to see where all the dead shunters are buried. I didn't like it very much. Grandpa told me about one who'd been crushed between two engines, and another who'd had a leg taken off when a wagon rolled over him. You won't make me be a shunter, will you, mum?' he asked desperately.

Mother soothed him with a firm promise and a handful of Liquorice Allsorts. Ken was never eager to accept grandpa's invitation again.

My grandfather was very concerned about his bowels. 'Bowels, Nellie, you've got to watch my bowels,' was his constant exhortation to his wife, and it became a catchphrase in our family for many years. One Christmas my Aunt Lil was staying with us. She was a kind of courtesy aunt, being the wife of my mother's cousin Joe, and her best friend, and she always treated Ken and me as a real aunt should. Sometimes mum and Aunt Lil could be as mischievous as we children, and on this occasion they made up a concoction of a pound of black treacle, mixed with half a pound of Epsom Salts and a slab of parkin. 'Just looking after your bowels, dad,' they said as they presented it to my bemused grandpa.

The house contained a bathroom and an upstairs lavatory – it was a posh house for Toxteth – but grandpa did not like stairs and preferred to use the outside loo, 'going down the yard' he always called it. Sometimes on winter evenings he would annoy the grown-ups and terrify us children by rolling up the evening paper and ramming it into the fire until it became a blazing torch. Then he'd rush 'down the yard', where he would shove the torch down the lavatory pan until the seat was warm enough for his requirements. He'd do this just as grandma had put a clean cloth on the table for supper, and the cloth became covered with smuts and bits of charred paper. Grandma complained bitterly each time it happened, but grandpa was a law unto himself and could never be prevailed upon to change his eccentric habits.

He had a phobia about catching cold, and constantly shouted, 'Shut that bloody door, that draught'll give me my death.' Before going out for his Sunday morning walk he would come downstairs in a heavy serge suit with a waistcoat and pullover beneath the jacket. Then he would pick up his muffler, warm it at the fire and wind it round his neck, tucking the ends inside his waistcoat. He then warmed his gloves and put them on, warmed the inside of his hat before putting that on, and as a last gesture he would warm the silver knob of his walking stick. Then he was ready for his walk. He insisted that grandma starched his collar for Sundays, and the hole the stud went through would get starched up too, making it difficult to get the collar in place. But grandpa would fight his collar furiously, losing his temper as usual. 'Lead, kindly light (go in, you bugger), amid th'encircling gloom (I'll teach you who's master in this bloody house . . .)' Then, if the stud still proved obdurate, he would tear off the collar, rip it into pieces and throw it on the fire. After waiting until he had calmed down grandma, muttering under her breath, would plod upstairs to get him another.

In his determination not to sit in a draught grandpa would huddle close to the grate in the kitchen, which was really like a large living-room, and stoke up the fire until the room was like a furnace.

One by one the family was driven out to cooler regions, leaving him in solitary splendour, a beetroot-coloured Shadrach revelling in his fiery pit. One of his heroes was Napoleon and he owned a biography which he read and re-read. With Napoleon in one hand and the poker in the other he attacked the fire savagely, at the same time mouthing the familiar words, happy at last and oblivious to anything that was going on around him.

One evening just before Bonfire Night Ken and I crept down from our room on the first floor and tiptoed to the kitchen. Grandpa did not notice our presence and continued to read and wield his poker. Ken, who could be a foolhardy little horror, with me usually following in his wake, sidled up behind grandpa's shoulder and threw a rip-rap into the fire. 'Rip-rap' was the Liverpool word for the kind of firework usually known as a squib, which is shaped like a little concertina and darts about all over the place, hissing and banging.

We shot out of the kitchen and into the hall and hid behind the door. The rip-rap exploded, leapt out of the fire and started its irregular course around the room. Grandpa stumbled to his feet and the firework chased him. 'GREAT JUMPING JESUS CHRIST!' he yelled, dropping the poker and hurling Napoleon across the kitchen. Then he heard our muffled laughter and realised what had happened. 'It's you, Ken, isn't it? Come here, you young bugger, and I'll tan the arse off you!' But we were upstairs and behind the locked door of our bedroom before he could take any action.

Grandpa liked the cinema and when we were not in disgrace would take Ken and me to the Rialto at the end of Prince's Road on a Saturday afternoon. We had to sit on the front row because he hated the smoky atmosphere and coughed ostentatiously if anyone smoked a cigarette near him. In those days sitting in the front row meant that the figures on the screen seemed about seventeen feet tall and three inches wide, and we would come out of the cinema with glazed eyes and stiff necks that lasted for the next two days. All during the performance grandpa smoked a filthy old pipe, managing to poison the air all around us, but his pungent blue smoke was perfectly acceptable to him, and complaints from people sitting behind us were disregarded.

In his later years, when his legs were wobbly, he did not go out very much. There was a lady living up the street, a kindly old soul called

Mrs Lee, who used to visit him twice a week with the intention of cheering him up. Unfortunately Mrs Lee was stone deaf and talked in fits and starts in a high loud voice that was without any modulation. Grandpa hated her visits but it was impossible to convey the fact to her.

'Here's Mrs Lee to see you, Isaac,' grandma would say, ushering the old lady into the kitchen.

Grandpa twisted his features into a ghastly rictus of pretended welcome while saying, 'Good Christ, what's she come for again? Hello, Mrs Lee, do come and sit down.' Mrs Lee would sit close to him and start bawling away. Grandpa's face, wreathed in smiles, grew more like a demented wolf's. 'Nellie, get her out of here,' he would say between clenched teeth, 'she's driving me mad!' But Mrs Lee stayed for her full half hour, and left convinced that the old gentleman had been immensely cheered up by her ministrations.

'Henry Irving will never be dead while you're alive,' grandma frequently told him.

As I have said, my mother, his only daughter, was the one member of the family who would stand up to him and give as good as she got. When she became twenty-one she was given a small party in the house. She and my father were courting at the time so naturally he was present. Grandpa was playing the gracious host and being unconvincingly congenial. 'Now, Nellie,' he said when she was being given her presents, 'it's your twenty-first birthday, here's a golden sovereign for you,' and he held it high so that everyone could see how generous he was being.

'Thank you, pa,' my mother said, surprised but gratified, and tucked the coin in her pocket.

When the party was over and all the guests had gone grandpa went up to her and held out his hand. 'Well, Nellie,' he said, 'you can give me the sovereign back now.'

'What do you mean, give it back?'

'Now, lass, you know I didn't really mean you to have it for keeps – it was only for show.'

'Show or not, I'm not giving it back to you. You've got a cheek, dad!' my mother said firmly, and he never did get it back.

Poor grandpa – he could not have been very happy. I often wonder what made him so fierce and bad-tempered. There must have been some big disappointment in his life that none of us knew about. It could not have been grandma's fault. Though she never was a bundle of laughs she was a decent, hardworking and respectable body, inclined to grumble, but a good wife according to the conventions of the day. Grandpa died in 1946, when I was twenty, and the house became unnaturally quiet. For a long time even those of us who were not living at home missed his rages, his oaths and illogical actions. I don't think grandma ever got used to being without him. The absence of that loud voice brought on a strange restlessness, and she died two years later of a heart attack.

CHAPTER 3

Golden Times

WHEN we were living with my grandparents there were three uncles at home. Another was married and living elsewhere, two others had died in infancy. Uncle Harold, who worked at a printer's, was mad about wireless and his hobby was making wireless sets. The dresser was permanently festooned with valves and wires and on the fire there was always a pot of fish glue that stank the whole house out. Uncle Bill was a postman. He played the violin, had a good tenor voice, and appeared in local operatic performances. He died in 1930, never having fully recovered from the effects of being gassed in the First World War. Uncle Walter, who went to London to do something in insurance, played the piano, and he, Uncle Bill and a baritone friend formed a musical trio, their repertoire being drawn chiefly from light operas. Other friends came to the house and performed their pieces, vocal or instrumental, and the air was full of music.

Ken always showed more interest than I did and was always more critical. Sometimes we were allowed to stay up and be part of the audience as long as we sat quietly on the sofa. But it was difficult to maintain a serious listening pose when one rather thin lady performed 'I shot an arrow . . .' which, I think, belongs to a baritone. She trilled while making appropriate shooting gestures, eyes closed, rising on tiptoes for the higher notes and opening her eyes, perhaps, as Ken suggested, to get a better sight of the target. On occasions like that it was impossible not to give way to giggles, and though we suppressed them as best we could we usually finished up digging each other in the ribs, with tears streaming from our eyes and hankies stuffed in our mouths. Then we would be taken out by our embarrassed mother and given a good talking-to.

These gatherings took place in the cellar. A previous owner of the house had put down a good polished wooden floor and as well as music there was dancing to a gramophone. My uncles and their friends waltzed, foxtrotted and one-stepped to the popular music of the day. Nobody could afford alcohol at these little parties; home-made lemonade was the usual drink, but there was occasionally a bottle of port, sherry or cider, mainly at Christmas time.

At one of these musical evenings Ken came to me and said, 'Come and look what I've found.' I followed him to the back cellar which was also the washroom, with a brick copper, mangle, dolly-tub and other impedimenta; and from behind the copper he produced a bottle filled with a dark red liquid. 'Grandma must have put it there,' he said. 'Have some, it's good, it's like cherryade.'

I took a sip and it did indeed taste good, though very different from the drink I was used to. Then Ken took another sip, and so did I, and as the evening progressed we frequently crept to the back cellar and retrieved the bottle with its rapidly decreasing contents. I began to feel sleepy and my legs wouldn't work properly, so I crawled upstairs and curled up in a corner of a sofa in the parlour, cheeks flushed and eyes drooping. The drink had the opposite effect on Ken. His eyes sparkled and he pranced around, dodging between the dancing couples in the cellar, singing loudly but still tunefully the words of the song coming from the gramophone.

Soon afterwards grandma took my mother aside to the back cellar, and said in worried tones, 'Somebody's been drinking the port – there's hardly any of it left,' and she held up the almost empty bottle.

'Surely it can't be anybody here,' my mother said. 'They're not that class of person – ' Then, remembering Ken's antics, she had a sudden wild surmise. All that frenetic capering was unusual – and Jean was very quiet, where was she? She hurried up to the parlour and found me on the sofa, out cold, a state I remained in for twelve hours. My first drunken spree ended with a headache and a prolonged bout of sickness. My mother considered that my hangover was punishment enough as she guessed that I had not instigated the prank, but Ken had to undergo more severe treatment. He was made to give up his penny a week pocket money in order to pay for another bottle of port. However, after about three weeks mother seemed to have forgotten the whole episode and the penny was automatically restored.

Just around the corner from Arnold Street was Warwick Street where there were some marvellous shops. Preston's, a home-made cake shop, was one of the most exciting. The cakes were expensive by our standards so we rarely got to sample the cream horns, the Swiss rolls that oozed jam and the Eccles cakes stuffed with syrupy currants. Our eyes were often glued to the shop window, mouths watering but pockets empty. Another occasional treat was a fourpenny dollop of home-made ice cream from Malabar's, the dairy, which we fetched in a basin. I have never tasted ice cream like it since; its heavenly flavour has never been reproduced anywhere else.

The shop we usually patronised was Allen's sweetshop as they had a Sweet Club. When we were given a penny by an uncle, or for running an errand for grandma, we would deposit it in the Club. As the year advanced we would frantically try to calculate how much we could withdraw at Christmas. It was usually about two shillings and threepence which to us was a small fortune. Just before Christmas we would go to Allen's, full of expectation, present our Club card which recorded the amount we had saved, and then spend at least an hour choosing what to buy. The assistants were so patient; never a sniff was heard nor an eyebrow raised in exasperation. It was a pennyworth of this and a ha'porth of that, pointing to this bottle or that shelf and prowling around the shop in an agony of indecision. Then we'd finally leave, each with a box full of different treats.

Pride of place always went to a Fry's or Cadbury's Selection Box, which contained a sample of all their different products – a few chocolates and little bars of plain, milk or nut chocolate. Then there were liquorice bootlaces, sherbert dabs, humbugs and gob-stoppers, those curious coloured balls that revealed a different colour every time you took a few more sucks, Everton toffee, and the wonderfully named Sharp's Eaton toffee which gave rise to our most popular joke ... When we got home we had, of course, to taste this and try a little of that, offer mum and grandma a chocolate (a little reluctantly, perhaps), and pretty soon the Sweet Club box was empty, and all there was to look forward to was the sugar pig on Christmas Day.

My parents' ability to scrimp and save was amazing. If mum had a shilling or so left over from the housekeeping money she would go straight down to the Co-op in Park Road and put it in the bank; and there would be enough saved for us to go to Rhyl every year for a week's holiday. This must have meant a real sacrifice for dad because he did not get paid for holidays. But he never complained about being hard done by. He was keeping the family's head above water, even if it was only by an inch, and that meant everything to him.

We stayed at the same boarding-house in Rhyl every year, not one of the elegant ones on the front, but a less expensive one in a side street. Everything was a bit threadbare but it was as clean as a new pin – or mother would never have considered entering its doors. We got breakfast, but had to buy the provisions for the evening meal ourselves and take them back. The landlady, Mrs Lappin, would then cook the meal for us. The use of the cruet was included in the rent. 'Use of cruet' was quite an advertising feature of seaside boarding-houses.

Rhyl was a splendid place for children in the 1930s and we loved every minute of our holiday. The sandy beach seemed to be made specially for us, and the word 'pollution' was not in anybody's vocabulary. There was a paddling pool and a swimming pool and – something I have never seen anywhere else – a bicycle ring. Just off the promenade was a large concrete area with a bit of garden in the middle. We could hire bicycles in a nearby shop, they were wheeled across the road for us and taken to the 'ring'. Then round and round we would go. There were two-wheelers and three-wheelers, and by the time I was seven I was riding a two-wheeler, but Ken was still on three wheels. I don't know why, for he was stronger and more adventurous but perhaps just because I was a weak female I had to show off and try to prove that strength and gender did not always win. We would have been on the bicycle ring all day had it not been beyond our means – it cost sixpence an hour.

I wonder if people remember Lobby Lud? His whereabouts at various seaside resorts was a feature of the old *News Chronicle*. A picture of him with his trilby hat concealing most of his features would appear in the paper, and the place and time of his appearance would be announced. Anybody who spotted the mysterious figure could challenge him with a formula of words that had to be strictly adhered to, and if the challenger got it right he received five pounds. You had to be carrying a copy of the *News Chronicle* at the time.

One day we were sitting by the swimming pool when my mother suddenly leapt up. 'Look – over there!' she said excitedly.

'Over where? What's up?' said dad.

'There!' mum repeated. 'I'm sure it's him . . . Lobby Lud . . .'

My cautious dad shook his head. 'I shouldn't think so.'

'No, I'm *sure*,' said mum, staring intently at the nondescript figure. 'Come on, Archie, give me your newspaper. I'm going to challenge him.' For some reason she whisked me along with her and, with my feet hardly touching the ground, we ran after the man, across the sand and up the steps to the promenade. He was looking in a shop window when we caught up with him. Mother plonked herself in front of him and held out the newspaper. 'You are Lobby Lud,' she gasped. 'I read the *News Chronicle* and I claim the five pounds.'

The man let her get to the end of her piece and then said, 'I'm sorry, madam, I'd love to be Lobby Lud for you but I'm afraid I'm not.'

I shall never forget mum's disappointment and the dejected way we returned to dad and Ken. If she had won the five pounds we could have stayed on in Rhyl for another week . . . Dad had the good sense not to say, 'I told you so.'

We shared one room at Mrs Lappin's. Mother and father had the big bed and Ken and I had a little one each. Mother and I did the day's shopping in the morning while dad and Ken walked up and down the promenade, and we'd take the groceries back before starting the day's activities. Mrs Lappin's front door was locked at ten o'clock every night. I don't know what would have happened if we had returned a few minutes late after our evening stroll because we never dared to challenge the rule. No drink on the premises was another edict, but sometimes, very daringly, we would sneak in a bottle of cider. The aura of guilt that shone round our heads should have alerted Mrs Lappin. Next day we would smuggle out the empty bottle in mum's beach bag and deposit it in someone else's dustbin.

If the weather was wet, and once or twice we had a week when it rained every day, it was very difficult to fill in the time. After breakfast Mrs Lappin's boarders were not allowed back into the house, apart from delivering their groceries, until supper time. No sitting in the lounge listening to the wireless. We had to be out all day. So we would sit in a glass shelter on the promenade, with other people in a similar situation, all trying to avoid the driving rain. Dad read his paper, mother clasped her handbag and looked out to sea; and Ken and I, bored and restless, bickered endlessly and irritated the grown-ups. If there was no rain but a strong cold wind we would sit on the beach in a little huddle of basket chairs. There at least, wrapped up like Eskimos, we could make sand castles.

One of the main attractions at Rhyl for Ken and me was the fairground, especially a big marquee with an open front called *On the Farm*. The inside of the marquee was built like a garden with sloping paths twisting through the artificial grass and tired-looking bushes. It cost threepence to hire a horse, a pony I suppose it was, but it seemed as high as the heavens to me. The animal, with an excited but fearful rider on its broad back, clutching the reins as though the horse was just about to leap over a deep chasm, would wend its stately way up and down the gentle slopes until it had made a circle round the marquee, so that we ended up where we had started. I suppose the ride did not last longer than five minutes, but I enjoyed it more than I did a donkey ride on the beach. There was something so grown-up about it – sitting astride a real horse – and my imagination changed the mangy old beast into a galloping white steed usually only found in fairy tales.

It was 50 years before I rode a horse again. Then I was on a cruise with my friend Joyce Kay. On one of the shore excursions we went to Petra, a two and a half hour journey from Akabar, followed by a twenty minute ride down a very steep and stony gorge on horseback. Joyce had not been on a horse before in her life. I remembered the 'training' I had had at Rhyl, and shuddered. But we mounted courageously and, led by Arab guides, rode triumphantly into Petra.

I have always loved ships which, being a Liverpudlian, is not surprising. There was also my father's intimate knowledge of them which must have affected me and I felt the romance of everything to do with the sea from a very early age. I longed to get aboard any ship at all – from great liners sitting in the docks waiting to set out on voyages all over the world, to the busy steamers plying between Liverpool and Belfast and the smaller ones bound for the Isle of Man.

My first experience of sailing was in the little ferry boats travelling to and from the Wirral seaside towns of New Brighton, Egremont and Seacombe. A trip down to the Pier Head brought on a tingling excitement. We had to go down the walkway to the floating landing-stage, the steepness of which was determined by the state of the tide, then wait at the landing-stage for the arrival of the *Royal Daffodil*. This famous little boat had more than earned its retirement to Liverpool after its gallant work during the First World War. Slowly and with great dignity it would crab alongside, bumping against the huge rope cushions that looked like Shock-headed Peters. The rope was thrown and threaded over the capstan and then there was an asthmatic creak and rattle as the gangway was lowered and passengers disembarked. It was agony to have to wait until everybody was off and we could go aboard, New Brighton our destination. Every crossing of the Mersey was an experience to be relished; even today I look back with immense pleasure to those early 'cruises'. Probably the greatest satisfaction I felt after joining *Coronation Street* was being able to fulfil my childhood dreams and go on a wonderful cruise in a luxurious ship.

All of which is a preamble to my experience of what I consider to be the most beautiful ship ever built, the *Queen Mary*. My dad had worked on the *Queen* when it was being built at the John Brown shipyard in Glasgow, and I was about seven when it sailed on its maiden voyage. It was in Southampton waiting for the great day and as dad felt he had a personal stake in its fortunes because of all the work he had done he decided that we should all go there to see her in all her pristine magnificence. Rarely having been further from home than Rhyl I was looking forward to a big adventure, and it started as soon as we set out from Lime Street Station. The train to London took four hours, chuffing through beautiful unfamiliar countryside, then we had to cross London to catch another train to the south coast and everything was so new and exciting I forgot how tired I was. We stayed in Southampton for a week, and that year the holiday was a substitute for Rhyl.

The best part of our visit to the *Queen Mary* was that we were privileged visitors. Not for us the crowds of tourists in organised charabanc parties. As dad was well-known as his firm's foreman he was allowed to be our escort, all doors were open to us and we saw parts of the ship that were out of bounds to the general public. At the forefront of my memory is the First Class swimming pool, huge and stunningly elegant. The pool itself was made from pale turquoise tiles, and that day it had been filled for the first time. The tiles seemed to shiver and shimmer with an almost hypnotic effect. The ceiling was done in mother-of-pearl mosaic and the milkiness was reflected in the blue water. Such beauty took my breath away. Even my practical-minded brother stood open-mouthed.

He was fascinated by the Children's Playroom in the First Class quarters where, round the four walls, a wide shelf ran on which were laid out the latest models of Hornby electric trains, narrow gauge rails with a complete complement of country scenes. There were all the points, signals, bridges, stations and taxis – everything to hold any child in thrall. Ken would have spent the whole week in that room if he'd had the choice.

The marvels were unending. There was an entire street of shops, a replica of Bond Street with its original shop fronts, all built along one of the decks. Although less than the size of real shops one could go in them and buy things. Travellers to America could actually have a suit made during the voyage; measurements were taken on the first day and the suit was finished by the time the liner docked in New York. Such service! How little the tailors would have seen of the patterns and colours of the ever-changing seascape.

When the ship was turned into a troopship during the war my father was understandably very sad. He knew it was inevitable but it still hurt to hear how the exquisite panelling had been unceremoniously ripped out and thrown into the Mersey. Fortunately, it was all replaced after the war when the *Queen Mary* returned to civilian life.

I have my own *Queen Mary* souvenirs – two brown bakelite ashtrays that a purser gave to dad. I still use one of them in my kitchen. Many people, though, will have rather more glamorous souvenirs which were not acquired as legitimately as my ashtrays. Dad told me about the things that were stolen when ships were being fitted. Once he was in charge of the fitting of wall switches in a row of cabins. One of his electricians did the actual work and after he had finished one row he went to dad's office to ask him to check the job. They went to the first cabin and found that the newly installed switch had disappeared, so had the next, and the next. Someone had been quietly following the electrician and removing each switch as soon as the workman had gone on to the next cabin. So they had to start all over again, this time with dad's eagle eye on the whole operation.

Other thieves on the *Queen Mary* were equally outrageous. In the First Class lounge there was a gilt clock in the form of a sunburst – a huge thing which weighed about half a ton. The electrician connected it up and made sure it was working, then went to find dad, who was working elsewhere. 'Hey, Archie,' he said, 'I've finished the lounge clock – will you come and check it now?'

They went to the lounge and discovered that there was no clock there at all. It had completely vanished from the ship and was never recovered. I wonder who still has a sunburst clock weighing half a ton on the sitting-room wall of their little bungalow!

The *Queen Mary* has, of course, long been retired from sailing the Atlantic, and though I have not seen her myself, friends tell me that this queen of ships, moored at Long Beach in California, sits like a slightly dingy dowager bemused by her new role as a floating conference hall.

CHAPTER 4

Where it all Began

WHEN dad was working locally he would sometimes take us to the Pavilion Theatre. This was usually on a Friday because we did not have to go to school the next day and we could stay up a little later. We always went to the first house because we could get in without booking. Now I see that was where it all began, where I fell in love with the theatre; a love affair that I could not then explain and which I kept secret from everybody. Even then it was precious to me and there was no way I was going to be laughed at. Little Jean, skinny, crop-headed, scabby-kneed, standing on a stage and making people laugh, or cry – it would have been too absurd. But not to me . . .

Sitting in the pit, with the lights going down, the footlights on the tatty red velvet curtain with the gold fringe which was just about to rise, the orchestra coming to the end of the overture – that was it! Excitement, happiness, longing, were all mixed up in me; and though I enjoyed everything that followed there was nothing to equal those first few heart-stopping moments.

Though our visits to the Pavilion were infrequent we saw a great number of acts over the years. Billy Bennett, Cavan O'Connor, Lucan and McShane, the Four Charladies, Randolph Sutton, Dorothy Ward and Shaun Glenville in pantomime – all these were among the stars but there were always lesser lights on the bill to provide fun and excitement. There were jugglers, singers, trapeze artists, second-string comics, unicyclists, dogs and doves. I would watch the chorus girls and sigh because I thought that what they did was very difficult and needed a lot of practice, especially when they had to dance balancing on large rubber balls. I remembered those I'd seen at Mrs Allington's and would reluctantly decide that I hadn't got the talent or the stamina to be a dancer. And though the comedians made me laugh till I was breathless, even when I could not understand half the jokes, I knew that I could never have the confidence to be a Nellie Wallace or a Suzette Tarri. As for the singers – well, I could not sing in tune, or so everybody told me, so singing was out. And I couldn't keep three balls in the air, or hang by my teeth from a swinging bar, or produce a rabbit from a hat, or play the clown like Stanelli and his Hornchestra, so what could I do? It seemed that my career in the theatre was going to be short and uneventful.

Then one night we saw Teddy Brown, an enormous American, all girth and smiles, who played the xylophone. He did not have to speak or move as he could reach either end of his instrument without stretching his arms. He beamed away, banging on the keys with his little hammers, sometimes doing an aimless shuffling dance, and I knew then, without any doubt, that that was what I was going to be – a female Teddy Brown. What an easy way to earn a living! But afterwards I began to wonder just where in Toxteth could I learn the xylophone, how would I acquire one in the first place and where would I keep it? Sadly my little bubble burst and I came down to earth. But it would have been an ideal occupation, and Teddy Brown still remains my first inspiration.

Less glamorous entertainment than the Pavilion provided was to be found in Rhyl at the open air Pierrot Show on the promenade which was run by 'Uncle Billy', who was a genial old man whose company numbered six, apart from the pianist. Even to my young and untutored eyes I could see that they were not in the same class as the acts at the Pavilion, but I enjoyed their unsophisticated entertainment enormously. I used to go in the 'scotch seats' – the free ones, not the deck chairs, for which you had to pay. Behind the deck chairs was a barrier on the other side of which you could stand and see the show. In the interval a member of the company would come round the scotch seats with a collecting-box. Many people would then sidle away, pretending they had an important engagement somewhere else, but I always managed to put at least a ha'penny into the box because I was too ashamed to watch the show without paying anything. And, in any case, it was worth a ha'penny. Every afternoon, about half past two, I would be at Uncle Billy's, worming my way between people's legs so that I could get right up to the barrier. Mum and dad always knew where to find me if I suddenly disappeared.

And so my interest in the theatre continued to grow quietly and slowly in that special corner of my mind, and nobody guessed my secret.

The main road in Toxteth was Prince's Road. The backs of the houses faced the backs of the Arnold Street houses, with a narrow street called Pomfret Street separating them, and it was quiet enough for children to play in it safely. When I was about 12 my two best friends, Pauline and Rose Simmons, lived in Prince's Road. We went to school together and met each other in the evenings when homework was done. Their family was Jewish – large, gregarious and welcoming. I felt as though I had a second home when I was with them. They had a cousin named Marion who lived with them; she was eight years younger than the rest of us and we very much resented having to take her around with us. She was a four-year-old baby while we were twelve-year-old grown-ups. So we tried dodging away from her, disappearing round corners or up alleys. But 'I know you're there!' Marion would shout, then, more plaintively, 'Where are you?' as she tried to follow our uniformed backs.

When the war started in 1939 the two older girls were evacuated to Canada and I lost touch with the family and Marion, who was still too young to be counted as a proper friend. Eventually I left Liverpool and, many years later, I landed up in *Coronation Street* in 1964. Two years after that I was asked to make a charity appearance at the Queen's Hotel in Southport to accept a cheque for the Christie Cancer Fund, the money for which had been collected by the local Jewish Ladies' Guild. Almost the first person I saw when I entered the hotel was Marion, sitting at a table with her mother. We instantly recognised each other after 27 years, fell into each other's arms, and have been good friends ever since. Marion, the four-year-old child who called 'Where are you?' is now a doctor's wife with grown-up children of her own, and she has forgiven me for having given her so many anguished moments all those years ago.

Though I was not intellectually brilliant I worked really hard at primary school and won a scholarship to St Edmund's College in Devonshire Road. Two years before that Ken had gone to Liverpool Institute, one of Liverpool's finest boys' schools, where he shone at Classics. Our paths had diverged naturally; he congregated with his chums, and I with mine and, with two years between us, we moved in different circles, though both his friends and mine would meet at our house. But although our interests were no longer shared we remained on good terms and frequently presented a united front to an occasionally hostile world.

St Edmund's College was a girls' school just on the edge of Prince's Park, and there was a back way from the school grounds into the park where we used to go for tennis lessons once a week. We younger girls preferred to use the lower court which was surrounded by a high hedge because if the games mistress was on the upper court she could not see what we were up to. And one of our hidden and forbidden delights was drinking beer! It was only nettle beer, actually, not particularly alcoholic, but we thought we were wild spirits to be drinking it on the quiet. It was made by the mother of one of the girls who smuggled great jars of it into the park. We would bounce a tennis ball around and shout out imaginary scores while sitting on a bench drinking the foaming liquid. One girl would always be on guard in case the mistress decided to leave the real tennis players and see what the rabbits were doing, so we were always earnestly serving or returning when she appeared from behind the hedge.

I did well at St Edmund's and usually managed to finish in the first four in form position. I particularly enjoyed English, due to the enthusiasm of Miss Potter, who was mad about Shakespeare and succeeded in making me mad about him too. Not only did I enjoy reading Shakespeare in class but I would continue in the evenings. In fact I got so obsessed that I sometimes used to go to the house of my friend Rene Edwards, and together we eventually read through every play, taking alternate parts and getting mixed up when there were more than two people in a scene. But in spite of our limited experience our imaginations were unlimited and we managed to make Portia, Cordelia, Viola and Rosalind really come to life in that small bedroom, along with Prince Hal, Falstaff and Hamlet. The task took some years, and when we had closed the book on the last scene of the last play we both felt thoroughly deflated. So we started on the Sonnets . . .

Miss Potter apart, most of the other teachers have become dimmed by time, although Miss Leatham stands out. She taught French and took our class when our regular teacher was absent. She was very earnest, very mild-mannered, and was besotted by cats. So if we did not feel like wrestling with French verbs one of us would ask her innocently, 'How's your cat, Miss Leatham?' She fell for it every time! The rest of the hour passed pleasantly, Miss Leatham enlarging on the personality and habits of her beloved Tarquin, while we talked behind our hands, ate sweets or read *School Friend*.

St Edmund's used to have an annual concert when parents would come along to see their offspring perform and would go away filled with pride. Truthfully, it was rather dull, consisting chiefly of narrative poems and *Nymphs and Shepherds*-type choral items which were rather raggedly performed. St Edmund's was a church school and inclined to be staid, and that type of programme was thought to be most suitable for respectable young ladies, though we found it hard to stifle the occasional yawn during the lacklustre proceedings. During my last year at school the inspirational Miss Potter decided to challenge the established scheme of things. 'Do you think we could change the style of the concert?' she said to us one day, after a particularly stimulating English lesson during which we had all reached new heights of histrionics. 'It would be so nice to do something different.'

We agreed wholeheartedly, and after Miss Potter had cleared the idea with a somewhat doubtful Miss Hennings, the headmistress, a few of us got together to plan the innovations. We wrote some sketches, we livened up the choice of poems, and even wrote some of our own, all of which met with Miss Potter's approval. She was especially pleased when we asked if we could end the concert with a one-act play. We decided on Stanley Houghton's *The Dear Departed*, a broad old-fashioned comedy. I did not have a part in it but was very pleased to be asked to direct it. The new style concert and the play were received with great enthusiasm, even by the headmistress, and Miss Potter congratulated us all, obviously very relieved.

My wish to act was fulfilled very soon afterwards. A few friends from Sunday School and I formed a little acting group to perform one-act plays in halls in our area for such charities as Church Roof Funds, organ repairs and Christmas parties for pensioners. One of the plays was *The Dear Departed*, chosen by me so that I could re-live my directorial triumph and also give myself a part – that of Ma. Thereafter I seem to have spent most of my acting life playing Ma's! That first part in a real play before a real audience put the seal on my ambition and my determination to be an actress.

Miss Potter took our form to see our first Shakespeare play at the Royal Court Theatre when I was 15, and what a wonderful introduction it was: John Gielgud and Gwen Ffrangcon-Davies in *Macbeth*. I came out of the theatre in a trance and could not speak all the way home.

The next year I started going to see Donald Wolfit, whose annual visits to Liverpool stretched over six glorious weeks. Wolfit would bring four or five plays each time, and I can remember seeing *A Midsummer-Night's Dream*, *Othello* and *The Merry Wives of Windsor*. I soon became accustomed to Wolfit's idiosyncrasies and looked forward to them, but most of all I loved to anticipate his curtain speech which was often the best performance of the evening. Whatever he had been play-ing, Bottom or Lear, he would appear for his call practically fainting with exhaustion. Sometimes he would hang on to the curtain as though unable to stay upright a moment longer. I loved this final touch of ham acting as much as I admired his dedication to Shakespeare.

At this time I was studying for my School Certificate, the equiva-lent, I believe, of O Levels. During the early summer the Chanticleer Theatre Company was playing at the Open Air Theatre in Otterspool Park. Every night I would collect my books, get on my bike and cycle to Otterspool which was quite a few miles from home. Weather permitting, I would sit on the grass and munch a sandwich and an apple while trying to cram into my head as many relevant facts as I could for the following day's exam. Then I would see the play. They did three plays in the fortnight: *St Joan, The Taming of the Shrew,* and *Love's Labour's Lost,* and I never missed a performance. I would go every night during their short season even if it meant seeing one play over and over again. I really do not know how I passed my exams. I did manage to scrape through, but I'm sure I learned more from watching the plays than I did from stuffing my head with facts which I had forgotten as soon as I had left the examination room.

CHAPTER 5

A Schoolgirl's War

IN 1939 the even tenor of our schooldays was broken dramatically by the outbreak of war. This was at the beginning of my second year at St Edmund's. The authorities decided that because of the danger of the docks being bombed the whole school should immediately be evacuated to – of all places – Chester. You could walk there from Liverpool – well almost! But it took four hours by train. The day before war was declared was a Saturday and all four hundred girls were put on a train, the destination of which nobody seemed to know. Certainly we girls didn't. Our parents took us to Lime Street Station, and there were distressing scenes of farewell as we got on the train, each of us with a gas mask in a box, a small suitcase with a change of clothing, and a label in the lapel. I'm sure we all thought we would never see our mums and dads again.

The train chugged out of the station, snuffled through the blackened Edge Hill tunnels and crawled all over the countryside until at last we landed up in Chester. Liverpool was, of course, a potentially dangerous place to be in. It was full of servicemen who had been mobilised and were waiting in ships standing in the river ready to be sent off all over the world, and it was quite likely that the enemy knew this. They probably also knew that Chester had the overspill of troops because it was the nearest town where they could be adequately billeted. Chester Castle had the Argylls; and Sealand Aerodrome, where the R.A.F. trained, was only a mile outside the town. Sailors waiting for embarkation roamed around the town in their hundreds, so Chester was scarcely safer than Liverpool.

We girls were billeted all over the town, in ones and twos, sometimes made welcome and often not. I was one of the lucky ones, being dumped on a couple who could not have been nicer. Our form mistresses had to traipse round the town every night to make sure that we were all where we should be. We were not allowed to go out in the evening on our own, which was a sensible rule, though not always observed by the older girls. And to make matters more chaotic we all used to return to Liverpool by bus every Friday and go back to Chester on Sunday night. Things got to the stage when nobody seemed to know who was where and what was what, and at last bureaucracy yielded to commonsense. We left Chester for good and returned to Liverpool at Christmas.

For a schoolgirl it was an exciting rather than a frightening experience, though food rationing and queues for such things as onions and knicker elastic were boring. Arnold Street never got a direct hit. For some reason whatever the enemy sent down seemed to jump right over us. From wherever the bombs came, seeking out the river and the docks, we would hear six loud bangs. If, after the sixth, Arnold Street was still standing, we knew we were safe for the time being, though all around us there was hardly a street that had not been affected at some time or other.

At five o'clock one dark and chilly November morning, with slushy snow on the ground, an air raid warden knocked on the door. We were then living next door to the grandparents in a house of our own. 'Everybody out!' he called.

'What's all this?' my mother protested, leaning out of an upstairs window.

'There's an unexploded landmine about half a mile away. Everybody's got to vacate their houses. Get a move on, missus, please,' and he moved on to the next house.

Then there was a little quiet panic. Mother gathered Ken and me together, then hurried next door to see that Uncle Harold was there to look after the grandparents. Ken ran upstairs to tell Mrs Peters.

Mrs Peters was very old, 80 at least, and had been staying with us since her last remaining son had got married just before the war and left home. She could not manage a large house on her own and knew we had a spare room, so had asked mother if she could stay with us.

35

The arrangement suited everybody and she was with us till she died at the age of 88. She was a straight-backed, straitlaced old lady, reminding us very much of Queen Mary, with white hair and long dresses that touched the ground. She had tremendous spirit and never showed any fear. We admired her tremendously.

'Please hurry, Mrs Peters,' Ken called.

The old lady appeared at her door. 'It's Sunday, isn't it?' she said. 'So I'll have to wear my best black.' She went back to her room and we waited in the hall below, biting our nails with impatience.

'Mrs Peters, this thing could blow us sky high any minute,' my mother moaned. 'We *must* go – '

The warden appeared again. 'Aren't you lot out yet? Do you want to get blown to smithereens? Come *on!*'

Mrs Peters descended the stairs slowly. She reached the hall and we gave a combined sigh of relief. 'I'll have to go back,' she said, 'I haven't got a clean lace and I've forgotten my handkerchief.' Her 'lace' was a modesty vest which she pinned inside the top of her frock to hide the slightest suggestion of a cleavage.

By this time mum was frantic. 'I'll get it, where is it?'

Mrs Peters was completely unruffled. 'In my dressing-table drawer,' she said. 'You'll find the lace and two little gold pins in a pot. The handkerchiefs are in the next drawer – '

My mother flew up the stairs . . .

At last Mrs Peters was provided with all her needs and we got out of the house and into the church hall where we were expected to spend the rest of the night. It was crammed with people and hazy with cigarette smoke. There was a pot-pourri of different smells, most of them horrid, and the floor was strewn with rather unpleasant-looking straw mattresses that the WVS had unearthed with their usual efficiency. Some people were trying to sleep, a group in one corner was singing. The WVS ladies were handing round cups of tea, there was the clatter of pots and cooking smells coming from the small kitchen; and the lavatories, one for each sex, had long queues outside them. I went outside for a moment and when I got back the stench hit me like a brick. But we had to stay there and eventually, encouraged by my mother, I lay down on a mattress and tried to get some sleep.

On the next mattress was an old man, and we could not help lying cheek to jowl because the mattresses were jammed together so closely. I was soon awakened by an unfamiliar sound, and to my horror saw that the tramp, for such he was, was having a jolly good scratch all over, legs, back, neck, head, *everywhere*. So I got up hastily and sat on a bench for the rest of the night. Mrs Peters was also sitting on a bench, her back as usual as straight as a ramrod. She was too arthritic to get down to a mattress, and I soon wished that I had been too stiff to bend when I found myself scratching my head . . . Grandpa, of course, also refused the indignity of a mattress, and spent the time glaring at everybody and muttering oaths.

In the morning we left the hall thankfully, drank in the clean air and stretched our weary limbs. The danger from the landmine was not yet over, but we had friends who lived at the other end of Prince's Road, outside the proscribed area, and they put us up until it was safe for us to return home. We stayed with them for a day and a night, and had to sleep in armchairs and on sofas; but anything was better than a tickly mattress and a smelly tramp. During that second night I read *Three Men in a Boat* for the first time, my enjoyment punctuated by the sound of bombs dropping and the mobile guns operating from a nearby Territorial Barracks, but even then I realised that it was one of the funniest books ever written. In calmer times I read it again and again, and I don't think I could be happy if I did not have a copy on my bedside table.

Coming home from school one day I found a tiny tabby kitten with a white shirt-front and white paws in a pool of water in the street. I picked up the little ball of soaked fur, listened to its faint mewings and, doubtless inspired by Miss Leatham's cat stories, I fell in love. This was not only with the tiny scrap in my arms, but with the whole cat kingdom; and today my life is dominated by cat sculptures, cat pictures, cat books – and the cats from next door. There must be an affinity between me and cats that only a psychoanalyst could explain – or perhaps I am the reincarnation of an Ancient Egyptian cat goddess. Mother, bless her, said that I could keep the pathetic little creature, whom I called Snooky and loved to distraction.

Snooky certainly earned his keep, in a very practical way, as an air raid warning. We had fitted out the cellars as a makeshift shelter with beds and chairs and we spent many nights in airless discomfort because when the bombs began to drop on Liverpool it seemed that they would never stop. The siren announcing a raid usually went off about seven o'clock. One night we noticed that, at about a quarter to seven, Snooky suddenly shot up from his cushion by the fire, scampered down to the cellar door and crouched there with his nose pressed against it.

'Whatever's the matter with him?' mother said, and went back to preparing supper, expecting dad home every moment.

Then without any warning there was a loud bang and a bombing raid had started. We all rushed for the cellar, each of us carrying part of the meal. Snooky was first down and under a bed. After that we would watch him every night, and if he made a move towards the cellar steps, even if there was no sound from outside, we would be there right behind him. Snooky could obviously hear something we could not, and whenever his ears pricked up it was a prelude to supper in the cellar.

There was great excitement one night in Pomfret Street, the road which divided us from Prince's Road. It happened in the garden of a house which faced our own back door and we became directly involved; at least, I did. The house had at one time belonged to a professor of music who had had a studio built at the end of his garden so that his pupils could perform to a wider public. After his death the studio became a night club and folks said that all sorts of things went on there in the evenings. I was never quite sure what 'all sorts of things' were, but my imagination made up for my lack of knowledge, and white slavery and dope were high in my feverish imaginings.

It happened for once to be an evening without a raid, but our peace was suddenly shattered by the sound of police sirens in Pomfret Street. In no time both ends of the street were blocked by police cars and American jeeps. It was dark and blackout regulations were in force so that we couldn't see very much and it was all very puzzling. My bedroom was at the back of the house so the family crowded into the room and we pressed our noses to the window. We could make out policemen with Alsatian dogs and American soldiers with guns drawn, a really frightening sight. I began to think that we had been invaded. I just had to get nearer the scene of the action. With no thought of danger I ran out of the house, hurried to the gate that opened into Pomfret Street and found a huge American soldier standing on the step with a gun trained on the studio opposite. Nearby was a jeep and a policeman with his dog.

'What's happening?' I asked, emboldened by displeasure at seeing our street being so desecrated by the trappings of violence.

'G.I. deserter – hiding in that club,' the soldier said, adding, 'Best go indoors, young lady, we don't want you getting into any trouble.'

At that moment Snooky appeared, rubbing against my ankle. He was usually a timid cat, but when he caught sight of the dog he shot straight across the road and under the jeep. There he stayed, back arched, tail like a flue brush, spitting at his new enemy. Fortunately the well-trained dog took absolutely no notice and kept his eyes fixed on the door of the night club. Snooky continued to shiver with rage, and I thought that if somebody didn't do something the dog's attention would be diverted to Snooky and he'd eat him. So I darted out into the road.

'Come back! You can't go out there!' the soldier yelled, his gun wavering in his hand, and I could hear shouting coming from the bedroom.

'I've got to get my cat!' I yelled back and was underneath the jeep before he could take any further action.

I finally caught Snooky and emerged with hands scratched by the furious cat and knees skinned by the hard road. As soon as I was back indoors, facing my parents' wrath, the whole street was suddenly lit up like Christmas, with headlamps and spotlights all focused on the studio, and soldiers were advancing with guns at the ready. I fully expected to see James Cagney or Edward G. Robinson creep out of the shadows into the full glare of the lights and play a part in the drama.

The anticlimax to the story is that the deserter was not in the night club at all. He was captured in another part of the town some days later.

The only time I ever saw my father out of countenance was during the war. Usually he was quite unflappable and nothing caused him to get excited. One night he was late home, at least half an hour after his usual time, and we were getting rather worried. He was working on refitting a ship in the docks which were being bombed incessantly. When at last we heard his key in the lock mother gave a sigh of relief and prepared to scold him. Then she saw how white and shaken he was and began to fuss instead. 'What's the matter? Are you hurt?'

'Just leave me alone and let me sit down,' dad said.

Eventually we got the story out of him. As all traffic used to stop when the raids started he had been walking home. When he was about three streets from home the raid was getting so heavy and noisy that he'd gone into a brick street shelter for about half an hour. When the bombing eased off a bit he decided it would be safe to make a dash for home. He had only gone a few yards when something whizzed past his nose and embedded itself in the ground in front of him. It was an eight inch long piece of shrapnel with jagged edges quivering. Half a second later it would have split his skull in two. 'Being so near death concentrates the mind wonderfully,' he said ruefully and was very thoughtful for the rest of the evening.

There was another time, however, when he came in laughing. 'I was coming out of the docks with Charlie Webster,' he said in explanation, 'when the raid started. There were bombs exploding all round so Charlie said, "Let's get under these wagons, Archie, they'll provide a bit of shelter until things ease up." ' So they crouched under a row of wagons on the dock road for about twenty minutes, as safe as houses, they thought. When they emerged from their shelter and looked around they discovered that they had been hiding under ammunition waiting to be loaded on to a ship the next day.

'It's no good worrying,' my father said, as so many people were saying in those dark and dangerous days. 'If it's got your name on it you've had it.'

CHAPTER 6

Marking Time

WHEN the time came for me to leave school at the age of 17 I was faced with the dilemma that so many young people were in. What to do? Of course I knew what I wanted to do, but, unlike going after a job in an office or classroom or behind a counter, there was no chance of me getting work in the theatre in Liverpool. I was totally inexperienced, had no influence, and, in any case, was at a loss to know how to go about it; though I did know I couldn't go to the stage door and say, 'Please, are there any jobs going?'

I was still too shy to share my secret ambition with anybody but my closest friends, but I had at least taken one practical step towards my goal by joining The Playgoers' Club, a well-established amateur drama club that Rene had already joined. I did a lot of useful work with them for a couple of years, listening, learning, getting to grips with some of the basic rules of an actor's work. I also became quite adept at stage management, set-building, the art of prompting and, perhaps the stage manager's primary function, taking the blame when things went wrong! I took elocution lessons too because it was essential, I thought, to lose all trace of my Liverpool accent. My elocution teacher was Mrs Ackerley at Crane Hall, and I paid her five shillings a lesson once a week. Years later I discovered that Peter Adamson had been at the school at the same time. I fondly imagined that I had acquired an attractively neutral way of speaking until I got my first professional job in the theatre when there was always someone who cut the ground from under my feet by asking, 'What did you say, Scouse?'

The job I finally did get was in the Liverpool Public Library Service as a very junior junior. One would have thought that, being a Shakespeare buff and fascinated by English literature, I would have been in my element among all those books. Not so! I worked in libraries for five years and hated every minute. It was boring and frustrating, and I could not see how my future as an actress would ever be achieved.

Soon after joining the service I was sent to the Co-ordination Department in Christian Street, off Islington. It was about as un-bookish a place as you could get, the department being responsible only for buying the books, invoicing them and distributing them to all the branches in the city. It meant that I had to learn to type, which I did quite quickly, though with a maximum of four fingers. I was frequently sent out as a relief librarian. For me the relief was getting out of the office but the purpose was to relieve hard-pressed staff when an assistant was off sick. There were 24 branch libraries and I could be sent to any one of them at a moment's notice. There were times when I worked very long hours for no extra pay. Typically, I would start work at Christian Street at nine o'clock, invoicing, perhaps, or preparing a requisition, only to be interrupted at ten o'clock with an order to go to some distant branch in the suburbs where someone had not turned up for work. Each branch library worked 'split shifts', that is, from nine to one, and five to eight. So if I was sent to the outer edge of the city I had to stay at the library till one, then I had to kick my heels for four hours, return at five and work till closing-time. I never knew how long I was going to work on any day of the week, but the hours were always what today would be called 'unsocial'. They certainly played havoc with my social life and contributed to my dislike of the job.

My time in the library service was considerably leavened by occasional trips to London with Rene Edwards to see as many plays as time and our pockets would allow. Rene had an uncle living in Dagenham and we took advantage of his standing invitation to stay there. We would travel to London on the night coach and then we walked everywhere, apart from getting into London from Dagenham on an early train, using a cheap workman's return ticket. During the day we would see all the sights, while excitement was building up inside us as theatre time approached. After the show we would fall asleep in the train back to Dagenham from both exhaustion and fulfilment.

One occasion was particularly memorable as it was the very last performance of the fabulous season at the New Theatre when Laurence Olivier, Ralph Richardson and their incredible company did *Henry IV, Oedipus Rex,* and *The Critic,* the last two in the same bill. The final performance of all was *Henry IV,* Parts 1 and 2: and Rene and I were there. Part 1 was performed in the afternoon, Part 2 in the evening. I had not managed to get a ticket for the evening perform-ance, much to my chagrin, not having been able to book in advance because of uncertainty about getting off work. Lucky Rene had a ticket, though, and I had hopes of getting a return. After the matinee I gave up thoughts of tea and took my place in the box office queue, on tenterhooks the whole time. But my hopes were dashed; by curtain up I still had no ticket and there seemed no chance of getting one.

Rene, equally anxious, had waited with me, but I persuaded her to go and take her seat. 'Don't, for heaven's sake, miss a moment!' I urged. I gestured to a sofa in the foyer. 'I'll sit here till the interval and you can come down and tell me all about it. It's better that one of us sees the show.' Rene saw the force of my argument and left me. The foyer had emptied and I flopped down on the sofa and tried to look inconspicuous.

After ten minutes or so, during which I grew progressively sadder, a man came out of a door next to the box office and approached me. From his demeanour and his dinner jacket I guessed that he was the theatre manager. He gave me a puzzled look. 'Have you come out? Are you ill?' he asked.

I stood up, rather embarrassed. 'No, I'm fine. It's just that I couldn't get a return.'

'Oh, dear,' he said. 'Then why are you still here?'

'Well, my friend did get a ticket – she's up in the gallery, and she has promised to come down in the interval and tell me all about it.'

'I see,' said the manager. 'I don't think we can have that on the last night, can we? Come with me, young lady.'

He took me up to the gallery and stood me at the back. 'You can stand there, and if anybody says anything to you, just refer them to me. Enjoy the play!' And with a smile and a pat on the shoulder he left me.

So, apart from the first ten minutes, I saw the whole play, and it was one of the great theatrical occasions of my life. And wasn't Rene surprised when, at the interval, I caught her just as she was about to run down the stairs . . . Many years later I had the pleasure of meeting Lord Olivier, as he is now, when he was producing and acting in a series of plays for Granada in Manchester. After I had been introduced to him and found him utterly charming I told him this story and of my undying gratitude to the manager. 'I'm not in the least surprised,' Lord Olivier said. 'That is precisely the sort of thing he would do. I remember him well – an extremely nice man. I'm glad you managed to see Ralph and me in the end. I hope you thought we did all right!'

It wasn't all unremitting toil in the library though, and there were some amusing moments. There was one library in Scotland Road to which I went regularly once a week. The librarian always had an afternoon off and his assistant finished at five, so I had to be there to take over till eight. In those days Scotland Road was a notoriously rough area, and even hardened Liverpudlians would shudder when 'Scottie' Road was mentioned. I was only 18 at the time and it was a lot to ask of a young girl to stay in the library on her own for three hours. But nobody in authority bothered about a little thing like that. On the whole, though, I coped well and was never aware of possible danger.

The library itself was a converted pub and had two sets of doors: two swing doors on the Scotland Road side, and the exit doors leading to a side street.

The Reading Room was partitioned off from the main library with wooden panelling. It was a large room and was always full, not only with legitimate readers but also with a regular crowd of homeless people who filed in the moment the doors were opened. They would take all the newspapers to use as sheets and would lie on the tables or benches and fall noisily asleep. At closing-time they were all turned out and would sit on the steps, hang about the streets or find a place to doss down; but in the morning they would all be there again, waiting for admission to their only haven.

I was always on my own behind the counter in Scotland Road, but I did have a helper to replace books on shelves, sweep up at night and distribute the papers and periodicals. He was a 14 year old streetwise, freckle-faced redhead named George. He was not very tall but he gave out an air of calm efficiency as he hurried around the library doing one of his many jobs, smart in his grey suit, and his carroty hair not very successfully slicked down with water. The official description of this tough little lad was 'runner', and as he more or less ran the place I had the utmost confidence in him.

One evening there was a terrific rumpus in the Reading Room, a thumping and drumming as though the vagrants had started another war. I was on my own, George having disappeared to the kitchen upstairs to make tea. Quickly I quelled my panic. I was in charge, so it was up to me – death or glory! I made a dash for the door but before I reached it George had come flying down the stairs. In an imperious manner he called out, 'Don't go in there, miss – you mustn't go in there!'

'But, George, there's a fight going on – '

By this time he was standing in front of the door, arms outstretched, guarding it like a latterday Horatio defending his bridge. 'No, miss, it's not a fight. I know what it is, miss, and I'll deal with it!' There were more frightening crashes. 'It's not for your eyes, miss!' Then he opened the door and firmly closed it behind him. I was left staring at the closed door wondering what nameless horror lay on the other side. Suddenly I realised that all was quiet in the Reading Room.

When George re-appeared, and settled me down with a cup of tea, he told me everything. Apparently one of the vagrants was an epileptic and regularly had a fit in the Reading Room. The poor fellow would fling himself about and everything went flying – chairs, tables, the lot – hence the awful din. George, no bigger than sixpennorth of coppers, knew precisely what to do on these occasions. He held the man down firmly, put something between his teeth to protect his tongue from injury, then got some of the man's friends to hold him until the fit was over and the exhausted man was quiet. Then George would lead him out to the fresh air, fetch him a glass of water, and leave him sitting on the steps until he was back to normal. The old man would return to the Reading Room, pick up his newspaper and carry on as though nothing had happened. This scene would occur every six weeks or so, and after a while the bangings and thumpings raised no more than an eyebrow from me. I knew I had a St George to come riding to the rescue.

There was a sequel to the story of the epileptic man. The Chief Librarian had a habit of popping into the library unannounced, unexpected and unwelcome. We knew, of course, that his snooping was to make sure that we were not skiving. One night, during my stint at Scotland Road, he arrived a quarter of an hour before closing time, when I was doing some preliminary cleaning-up. His eyes swept across the room, took in the counter, the file boxes, the book stacks, the notice board, and he appeared to be satisfied with what he saw. As he opened his mouth to speak, perhaps to congratulate me, the rumpus began in the Reading Room.

'Good heavens! What is that row?' he asked.

I was very calm. 'Oh, it's only an epileptic man having a fit.'

'A fit? And you on your own here? Oh, dear, how very . . . what do you do about it? Shall I – er – '

'Nothing to worry about,' I said cheerily, thinking to myself, 'Is this me talking to the Head Librarian like this?' Then I raised my voice. 'George will see to it.'

As if on cue George came bounding up from the basement, took in the situation, called out, 'Good evening, Mr Smith,' and shot off into the Reading Room.

Soon afterwards a slightly shattered Mr Smith made his departure, leaving me rather pleased at the way I had handled the situation.

Two days later I was at my desk in the Christian Street office when my boss called me into his room. He said, a bit uneasily, I thought, 'Miss Alexander, did you tell Mr Smith that a man has fits in the Reading Room?'

'Yes,' I answered.

'You should not have told him that,' he said coldly.

'Why not? He was there when it happened. What should I have said? That a fight had broken out? Wouldn't that have been worse?' I was amazed at the cool way I was standing up to him. 'Keep it up, Jean,' I said to myself.

'Er – no, of course not. I wouldn't expect you to tell lies.' (Oh, yes, you would, I thought!) 'But we don't like him to know about such things – it reflects on the staff when things go wrong. I'd be glad if you didn't do it again.'

I couldn't believe what I was hearing. 'What shall I do next time he has an attack? Let him die on the floor?' Anger gave my words a sarcastic edge.

My boss was silent. He looked down at his desk and I knew that the interview was over. I went back to my desk, fuming. I had already learned that life was not fair, but I thought this was ridiculous. I was never again allowed to be on duty alone at Scotland Road . . .

I did not always need George's helping hand and gradually learned to handle awkward situations myself. The little toughs of the neighbourhood were always a potential source of trouble, and it was vital to get the better of them from the beginning. This was not too hard for me because it was not all that long ago since I had been a bit of an urchin myself, and I knew most of the tricks. One evening two youngsters came in, and one look at their perky, bright-eyed faces told me that something was afoot. Now the good thing about these Liverpool back entry diddlers, as we called them, was that once you got the upper hand you earned their respect and they acknowledged that you were the boss.

On this occasion the bigger of the two walked boldly up to the counter. 'Want a form to join,' he said.

I gave each of them a form, told them to take them home for their parents to sign, and shushed them off the premises. A couple of minutes later they were back. They had each collected an assortment of rubbish from the street and wrapped it in a piece of newspaper. Without a word they hurled their parcels straight at me. I ducked and the nasty missiles went past my head. The boys had disappeared with the speed of light, but I knew what they were going to do. They would come round to the other door in the side street to see my reaction – there was no fun in perpetrating such a prank if they could not enjoy the result. I quickly left the desk and stood behind one of the swing doors through which they would enter. Sure enough the door opened and the two heads appeared, hoping to see me smothered in the contents of their bombs. They saw too late that the desk area was empty, but soon found where I was when I grabbed each of them by the scruff of the neck and banged their heads together. Then I flung them into the street. 'Don't you two ever come back,' I called after them, 'or you'll get more than a bang on the head!'

They took my words to heart, and news of my rough treatment must have got around after that for whenever little heads peeped round the door, I would hear, 'Don't go in – it's the red-'eaded one . . .'

A boy once returned a book, soggy and disgusting, and when I picked it up the spine fell off. 'You've been fighting with this book, haven't you?'

'No, miss, I ain't, miss,' he said, all indignation and hurt pride.

'What happened to the back of it, then?' I demanded.

'I dropped it, miss.'

'Dropped it? You mean, you hit somebody with it, didn't you? And you held the book by the cover, didn't you?'

He gave up the argument. 'How do you know, miss?'

'And you tried to stick the spine back on with – what on earth did you use for glue?'

'Conny-onny, miss.'

Condensed milk! So that's what the stickiness was on my hands – it was revolting. 'What on earth did you do that for?'

He seemed bewildered by my question; surely the reason was obvious. 'Because we 'adn't gorr any glue, miss.'

It was not only children who were sent to try us. Some of the adult readers required us to have the patience of Job and a sense of humour. A large and very harassed woman came in one day. It was a warm summer evening but she was not enjoying it. She waddled up to the counter and dumped two great shopping bags on it, scattering a heap of my papers on to the floor. She gave me her book and said, in the broadest of Liverpool accents, 'Jizz, girl, me feet's killin' me – go and find us a good love tale, cock.' So 'cock' would dutifully find her the latest Hebe Elsna, Vicky Lancaster or Lyndon Snow – all, had she known it, the same romantic novelist.

When the film of *War and Peace* was first shown in Liverpool everybody wanted the book of the film and there was a long list of readers who had never heard of Tolstoy but who had seen the film. I think the entire library service possessed only five copies, and these had to go out in turn from branch to branch. A little old lady came darting into the Scotland Road branch one day, waving her card triumphantly. 'Me book's in,' she cried, 'me book's in at last – can I 'ave it, girl?'

I took her reserve card – it was for *War and Peace*. The book was about six inches thick, on India paper, with small print. When she saw it her face dropped. 'God, is tharrit?' She felt its weight, opened it and looked at the tiny print. 'Oh, God, I couldn't read that,' she moaned. ''Ere y'are, girl, ta,' and she gave it back to me and scuttled out.

It was after a very hot August Bank Holiday weekend that I was due to go to the Everton library. Another junior and I trudged up the hill to open the library on Tuesday morning. I opened the door at nine o'clock and we were both immediately almost knocked backwards by the most appalling stench. It got worse every step we took and we thought that someone must have been inadvertently locked in the previous Saturday night and had died among the book stacks. We prowled around, keeping close together, but we could not find a body, so with great relief crossed 'corpse' off the list of possibilities. A more prosaic explanation was that the horrid smell must be coming from a book. Every librarian knows of the extraordinary things that people use as bookmarks – bacon rind, bus tickets, pension books, even, occasionally, a pound note – but this must be something special.

We started examining the shelves, stack by stack. It would be a formidable task to look inside every book in the library but we set to, and after three quarters of an hour I found it!

I pulled a book out of a shelf and it nearly fell apart in my hands. The middle was all green and crawling but I could just recognise what had been a kipper, now mouldy and disintegrating and, worse still, crawling with maggots – ghastly, stinking, death-coloured maggots which had been breeding profusely over the hot weekend. I deposited the horrid mess on a piece of newspaper then we hastily opened all the windows. I dumped the paper and its contents in a bucket of water and put it outside the back door. It was the rule for damaged stock to be returned to the Distribution Department where I guessed that it would fall to me to have to deal with it. Fortunately, when the librarian-in-charge came on duty he agreed that the book could be cancelled off our inventory and nothing more said. Very gracious of him, I thought . . .

I took a few exams during my five years in the service, though the time came when I rebelled and decided not to take any more. Each exam was in three parts, and only when you had passed all three did you get a pay rise – of five shillings a week! That meant it took about a year and a half to get through one examination.

I could see myself studying on and on into the distant future and all for an occasional miserly rise. At the age of 21 I was earning £11 a month. Surely life had more to offer than that! So I decided against going further with librarianship exams. I cherished the extra time I gained in not having to study, and in every spare minute I would rush into town, have a bun and a cup of tea at Lyons in Lime Street, then hurry to Williamson Square where I could stand in a queue for the gods for whatever was showing at the Playhouse. This happened at least once a week and was the only thing that kept me sane.

Among the plays I saw were *The Seagull, Arms and the Man, Romeo and Juliet, A Doll's House, Noah, Doctor Faustus, Twelfth Night, The Sulky Fire, The Master Builder, The Rivals, The Second Mrs Tanqueray, Anna Christie, A School for Scandal* and *Hamlet*. Could there be a more thorough grounding in great theatre?

While working in the library I had my 21st birthday. The war had been over for two years but rationing was still in force and lots of things were in short supply. My present from mum and dad was a meal in a restaurant for me and half a dozen friends. Eating out was unheard of in our family so it was a most exciting experience. A wonderful day came to a perfect end with a visit to the Playhouse to see *At Mrs Beam's*, a comedy by C.K. Munro, hopelessly old-fashioned, but our party found it very amusing. Years later I did the play in Rep.

I left the library service in the summer of 1949 when I was 22. I'd had enough, and had been ill again – pneumonia seemed to be my favourite illness, and I had to convalesce. As dad was working on a ship in Barrow mum and I went up to be with him and we stayed for nearly four months. Of course we went to visit Mrs Allington. She was very old then and no longer took in theatricals, but was as racy as ever and we were delighted to meet again.

By this time Ken had married and was teaching at Altrincham. He had finished at Cambridge in 1948 after a most successful course and had obtained a good degree. He had met Cynthia while they were both fire-watching during the war, he for his school, the Liverpool Institute, and she for the Art School where she was a student. The extra member of the family made us all very happy.

I did not enjoy my time in Barrow. The after-effects of the pneumonia took some time to shake off and I was out of work, with no immediate prospect of finding any. Although my parents put absolutely no pressure on me to go job-hunting, and they had not once reproached me for having given up a safe job with a pension at the end of a lifetime's service, I felt that they worried about my future and that added to my depression. How on earth was I going to get into the theatre?

CHAPTER 7

Professional at Last

THE answer to my dilemma came like a bolt from the blue – totally unexpected and totally heart-stopping, and my post-illness lassitude disappeared immediately. I have already mentioned Rene Edwards. She was my best friend at St Edmund's and we had remained close all through my library years. It was Rene with whom I had read Shakespeare two or three times a week for two years in her bedroom. We were also fellow members of the Playgoers' Club and together we had descended on the London theatre scene.

Rene got engaged to a mutual friend who had been with us in the Playgoers as a scenic designer. His name was Alexander Lyle but he was always known as Mac. Mac had recently got a job as Production Manager with a company called The Adelphi Guild Theatre which was based at Macclesfield. Rene followed to be near him until they could get married, and that, I thought, was the end of the story – goodbye to Rene. I would be friendless in Liverpool.

I was in Barrow at the end of July, 1949, still feeling sorry for myself, when a letter arrived from Rene. Amongst the chit-chat was the news that The Adelphi Guild Theatre was casting for a new season to begin in September. Mac had mentioned my name to Seumas Stewart, the Director of the company, as an experienced amateur who could work in all branches of the theatre and, if I liked, he would arrange an interview for me.

If I liked! My departure from Barrow was as swift as an eagle after prey, and in spite of my mother's 'But who are they? What are they?' I arrived in Macclesfield and sought out the company's office in

Chestergate, a dingy couple of rooms on the first floor of a far from elegant building. In the state I was in, calm on the outside but seething within, I would not have minded if I were to be interviewed in a hole in the ground.

The interview went well. Seumas Stewart, a gentle, scholarly Aberdonian, an ex-journalist and a Quaker, put me at my ease and let me talk. I prattled on all about the plays I had done, and all the plays I had seen, my backstage experience, about my determination from an early age to be an actress (I believe I actually mentioned Teddy Brown!), about Shakespeare, my favourite actors at the Liverpool Playhouse, and a dozen other things and, led on by an occasional friendly question, laid bare my quivering theatrical soul! I did not know how many other applicants Seumas had seen or was going to see, but he told me then and there that he thought I would be a valuable member of the company and could I start in September? I returned to Barrow in a trance; even my parents' guarded pleasure at my success did not drag me out of it.

The Adelphi Guild Theatre was a development of The Adelphi Players, founded by Richard Ward in 1941. Originally based near Colchester, it took plays to schools, hospitals, air-raid shelters, to the forces, war factory hostels, miners' institutes and, occasionally, proper theatres. The aim of the company was to take living theatre wherever it did not exist but was wanted. The members of the company, most of them pacifists, were enthusiastic and devoted, but not always practical, and the democratic set-up did not always work. Personality differences arose, there were clashes over the choice of plays and directors, there were fallings in and out of love, resignations, counter-resignations, and dramas off stage almost as intense as those on.

In 1947 there was a great split. Those members who wanted to continue the kind of work they had done during the war years went off to form another company of strolling players, but the majority decided to concentrate the work in the North Midlands so that they could settle down, make homes for themselves and raise families. The friendly Cheshire town of Macclesfield was chosen as the base, and there the company found it possible to develop both professional and domestic lives. The company was run on co-operative lines, with equal salaries for equal work (£5 a week!), without stars and without underlings, each sharing the fortunes of the whole and each equally responsible for the success or failure of the productions.

So I became part of a group of hardworking idealists. I seemed to fit in quite easily. I appreciated their friendliness and good humour though I could not always follow their philosophical discussions or join in their search for eternal verities. I had one close friend in Mac, and outside there was Rene, who was working in a shop in the town. She and I joined forces and took a bed-sitter in the YWCA. We were together for about a year, then she and Mac got married. He left the company to become an electrician and I stayed alone in the room we had shared.

My first play with the Adelphis was *The Hasty Heart* but, alas, there was no part for me in it. The only female part was given to another newcomer. I was the stage manager, a job more important and more difficult than anything I had had to do in my amateur days. The smooth running of the play depended on me – it was a frightening thought. However, I did not hesitate to ask for advice and very willingly it was given – the Adelphi company were a lovely lot of people, and unpompous in spite of their high ideals! I had to be on the prompt book, find or make the properties used in the play and help to set up and dress the stage every night. It was a tricky job, but I was so much in love with the whole set-up that I responded eagerly to the challenge.

I gained one unusual accomplishment during the run of *The Hasty Heart*, and one which so far I have not found any use for. One of the characters – Yank, played by Noel Lloyd – had, during one scene, to recite all the books of the Bible straight through without stopping. Being on the prompt book, I learned them myself without realising I was doing it. If Yank paused or gave the impression that he might 'dry' I could hiss the name of the book to him without having to glance at the prompt copy. When Noel and I meet these days we always start off our conversation with 'Genesis, Exodus, Leviticus, Numbers, Deuteronomy, Joshua, Judges . . .'

The next play was Somerset Maugham's *Sheppey*, and in it I made my first professional acting debut. It should have been the happiest experience of my life up to that time, but I find that in my diary I wrote

'Florrie – my God!' Florrie was the daughter of the family and the 'juvenile lead'. I knew I was not going to be very good as a sweet young thing because every part I had played with the Playgoers was one which needed characterisation; whether young, middle-aged or old, it had meat in it, and Florrie had nothing. I just could not simper, flutter my eyelids or gaze adoringly into the leading man's eyes. Such a character needed more acting experience than I had yet had, and my performance was as inadequate as I feared it would be. I did not like the play either . . .

We gave the play in the Library Theatre in Manchester and one of the local critics gave me the worst notice I have ever received in my life. The first and worst of forty years in the theatre! 'Incompetent' was the kindest word in it. My first reaction was to give it all up and rush home to Liverpool and hide away from the world, but then I mentally drew myself up to my full height and jutted out my chin defiantly. 'I *won't* let them get me down,' I resolved, and I never have. The reporter in question has since become a friend and a fan. I have reminded him how he nearly brought a promising career to a quick end, but he only smiles and says his review was an understatement!

As this was my first time away from home mum and dad had of course to come and see where I was living, what I was doing and who I was doing it with. First the YWCA was inspected and received the official seal of approval. Then they came to see the show; we were playing in Macclesfield that week. After the performance on Saturday nights it was customary for most members of the company to wind down with a celebratory drink at an unpretentious little pub near the theatre and I had started to go along with them – with some trepidation because I had never been in a pub before! Our family did not patronise them, partly because we could not afford to, and partly because my parents still tended to think a pub was a den of vice. My father's father had been a heavy drinker before being converted to total abstinence at an outdoor Salvation Army meeting (he turned out to be more unbearable sober than drunk). Mum did not realise where we were going until we reached the door of the pub, and then she was horrified. 'Jean,' she whispered, 'you don't go in pubs, do you?'

'It's all right, mum,' I tried to reassure her. 'We only come once a week for half an hour to relax.'

She probably wondered why we could not relax over a cup of tea but said no more and followed me in, though she clung tightly to dad's arm.

The pub was old, with low, smoke-blackened ceilings and oak beams, and was crowded. In the little room where we usually gathered were three elderly ladies sitting round a table that was littered with empty glasses and full ashtrays. One of them called over the barman and said, in a gravelly voice that sounded as though it had been kippered by stale smoke and an endless supply of stout, 'The usual, Herbert, three Guinnesses, I'll pay.'

My mother's eyebrows shot up in disapproval of these living witnesses to alcohol abuse, and I think she would have liked to turn round and march out immediately, dragging dad with her. But my friends took charge of them, saw that they were comfortable and chatted to them in an easy, relaxed way so that their fears that their only daughter had fallen into the clutches of the demon drink melted away. Dad accepted a beer and mother a port and lemon, and by the end of the evening I think she had decided that her very first visit to a pub had been surprisingly enjoyable! They left Macclesfield the next day, relieved of their fears and glad that I was happy.

The main feature of life with the Adelphis was the touring. We played one, two and occasionally three night stands within a radius of about forty miles, travelling in a huge silver van that carried scenery, props and, in a specially designed cabin above the front of the van, the members of the company. When we arrived at our destination my special job was to arrange the makeshift dressing-rooms, put out the make-up boxes, set up the lights and help the electrician – all that, of course, as well as act. I pride myself on having adapted quickly to such a strenuous programme. Unloading the van was frequently a traumatic experience. We would secretly pray that when we arrived at an unfamiliar hall the playing area would be on the ground floor, but it rarely was. So many of the stages, especially in town halls, were up flights of stairs, and the heavy scenery and skips had to be manhandled up narrow staircases and round awkward corners.

I got very good at carrying a 14 foot flat up a couple of flights at a rate of knots and after two years with the Adelphi I had muscles like a

Mother and dad's engagement photographs
(1917)

Grandpa Hill (1915)

Ken (aged 3½) and me (aged 1½)

Ken (aged 5) and me (aged 3)

Ken and me (aged 4) in hand-me-down jersey,
Barrow Park

Grandma Hill, mother and me (aged 8)

Me (aged 9)

Just after leaving the library service, when I
was 23 years old

With the Adelphi Guild Theatre at Macclesfield (1951)

My first professional appearance (1949)

Sheppey

By SOMERSET MAUGHAM

Sheppey	...	...	...	...	JOHN HEADLEY
Miss Grange	...	...	...	MARGARET MAXWELL
Bradley	...	...	...	...	RONALD SLY
Mr. Bolton	...	...	...	PIERS PLOWMAN
Albert	...	...	...	...	RICHARD JERRAMS
A Reporter	...	...	...	MALCOLM HOLLAND
Bessie Legros	...	...	...	BETTINA STERN
Mrs. Miller	...	...	...	PENELOPE BARRON
Florrie	...	...	...	...	JEAN ALEXANDER
Ernest Turner	...	...	...	LESLIE GODFREY
Dr. Jervis	...	...	...	...	NOEL LLOYD
Cooper	...	...	...	...	PIERS PLOWMAN

ACT 1

Bradley's Hairdressing and Barber's Saloon, in Jermyn Street, London, W.

♣

ACT 2

The living-room of Sheppey's home at Camberwell. Late Saturday afternoon. One week later.

♣

ACT 3

The same. Several days later.

THE PLAY PRODUCED BY SEUMAS STEWART

SETTINGS BY ALEXANDER LYLE

There will be an interval of ten minutes between each act.

COFFEE WILL BE SERVED DURING THE FIRST INTERVAL

Production Manager	ALEXANDER LYLE
Chief Electrician	TOM JELLIS
Wardrobe and Property Mistress ...	PENELOPE BARRON
Stage Manager...	RICHARD JERRAMS

The setting constructed in the Adelphi Guild Theatre Workshop.

With Noel Lloyd in *The Prince of Darkness is a Gentleman*, Macclesfield (1951)

Programme for *Uncle Harry*, Scala Theatre, Southport

PROGRAMME

Commencing MONDAY, 10th February, 1958, at the Scala Theatre

The SOUTHPORT REPERTORY Co.

presents

"UNCLE HARRY"

by THOMAS JOB

The Quincey Household

Hester Quincey	EILEEN DERBYSHIRE
Lettie Quincey	JEAN ALEXANDER
Harry Quincey	DONALD BODLEY
Nona	ELSPETH SEELEY

The Visitors

Lucy Forrest	BARBARA WHITTY
George Waddy	PETER SCHOFIELD

"The Bluebell"

Mr. Jenkins	PETER CLAYTON
Miss Phipps	MOIRA COLLIN
D'Arcy	VINT GRAVES
Albert	STANLEY LLOYD
Jimmy — Members of	DEREK BANCROFT
Mr. Blake — The Glee Club	STEPHEN THORNE
Ben	JOHN LOUKES

The Officials

The Governor	DONALD PELMEAR
Mr. Burton	CHRISTOPHER DYER
Eccles	MICHAEL SUMNER
Roberts	JULIE TAYLOR

PRODUCED by DONALD BODLEY

Settings painted by CORRINNE COOPER
assisted by BERYL BUNN and SUSAN JOHNSON

• If you enjoy the Play, tell your friends •

The action of the play takes place in a small town in the North of England.

ACT I.

Scene 1. Prologue - Epilogue. The Parlour of the Bell Tavern. August, 1912.

Scene 2. Tea - Time. The living-room of the Quincey's. September, 1908.

INTERVAL

ACT II.

Scene 1. Musical Interlude. The Parlour of the Bell Tavern. The same evening.

Scene 2. Night - Cap. The living-room of the Quincey's. Later that evening.

INTERVAL

ACT III.

Scene 1. Verdict. The Parlour of the Bell Tavern. December, 1908.

Scene 2. Confession. The office of the Governor of the Prison. January, 1909.

We are greatly indebted to the following for Properties used in this Production

Mrs. Aldam, Tulketh Street, and Mrs. Bain, Eastbank Street, and Metcalfe's, Lord Street, for Antiques.
Southport General Plating Co., Portland St., for Pewter Tea Service.
Timothy Whites, Chapel Street, for Umbrella.
Gas Showrooms, Eastbank Street, for Gas Brackets.

... NEXT WEEK ...

we present

A Play by RODNEY ACKLAND
based on a short story by W. Somerset Maugham

"BEFORE THE PARTY"

A big success when first staged at London's St. Martin's Theatre

This play has Comedy and Drama, and offers excellent acting opportunities to the cast.

BOOKING OFFICE OPEN 10 a.m. to 8 p.m. DAILY
YOU MAY ALSO BOOK BY TELEPHONE - 2426

As Marty in *Anna Christie*, Theatre Royal, York

A VIEW FROM THE BRIDGE

By ARTHUR MILLER

CHARACTERS IN ORDER OF THEIR APPEARANCE

MR. ALFIERI	JEFFERY DENCH
LOUIS	DONALD PELMEAR
MIKE	GEORGE HARLAND
EDDIE	JAMES BECK
CATHERINE, his niece	JUNE BARRY
BEATRICE, his wife	JEAN ALEXANDER
MARCO	DENNIS SPENCER
RODOLPHO, his brother	TREVOR BANNISTER
FIRST IMMIGRATION OFFICER	WILFRED BOYLE
SECOND IMMIGRATION OFFICER	TONY MORTON
MRS. LIPARI	MARGARET ROBERTSON
MR. LIPARI	RONALD PHILLIP
	CHERRY CREST
	BOBBIE OSWALD
NEIGHBOURS	PENELOPE HONOR
	DEIDRE DEUCHAR
	MARLENE PLESTER

The play produced by KEITH ANDREWS

Setting designed and painted by JANE DODWORTH *assisted by* BERYL BUNN

SYNOPSIS OF SCENES

The action takes place in the apartment and environment of Eddie Carbone, all in RED HOOK, on the Bay seaward from BROOKLYN BRIDGE.

The time is the present.

The play is in Two Acts
with an Interval of fifteen minutes

Interval music played at the piano
by DENIS NEILL

Stage Director: GEORGE HARLAND

Assistant Stage Managers	{	BOBBIE OSWALD
		PENELOPE HONOR
		TONY MORTON
Stage Carpenter		SYDNEY BURROWS
Chief Electrician		WILLIAM OGLESBY

We are grateful to the following for loaning furniture and properties for this production :
Bean & Whitehead, Colliergate. Grants, Coney Street. Plesters, Petergate. Nylon Stockings by Kayser Bondor. Bettys Restaurant, St. Helen's Square. The Church Shop, Tanner Row. Scobey's Garage, Bootham. The County Hospital. Hartnells, Market Street. Boultons, Coney Street. Leak & Thorp, Coney Street. G.P.O. Telephones. Cramptons, Toft Green. Oldfields, Davygate. Precious, Petergate. Naylors, Peter Lane.

Programme for *A View From the Bridge*, York

With Bunny at our special anniversary party to celebrate 10 years on The Street (1974)

With Bernard Youens and Sheila Price in *Arsenic and Old Lace* at Oldham (1975)

With my mother and brother Ken (1978)

navvy's! There was one occasion at Buxton when I took part in a sceneshifting race. There were some of the theatre's own stage-hands there to help us, and one of them pushed me out of the way just as I was about to lift up a flat, implying that a weak woman could not perform such a masculine task. 'You can't carry that,' he said.

'You want to bet?' I replied. 'I'll race you up the stairs with a 14 foot flat.'

The man gave a sceptical snort. 'You're on, mate,' he said. So we each took hold of a flat and I beat the hulking great brute with seconds to spare. 'I'll buy you a drink afterwards,' he gasped.

'No, I'll buy *you* one,' I replied, swaggering away, the honour of my sex vindicated.

I had not been with the Adelphis long before I began to be troubled by odd pains in the gut. At first they were rather vague, and as I had no time to go to a doctor I rather neglected the condition. Then the pains began to burn and I had bouts of sickness, not the usual rejection of stomach contents, but watery acids, and the trouble always manifested itself at an inconvenient moment. The most bizarre occasion was when we were returning one night along the road which passes *The Cat and Fiddle*, whose claim to fame is that it is the highest pub in England that keeps open all the year round. Sitting in the cramped space above the driver's cabin I suddenly felt one of my spasms coming on. I nipped down the steps to the main part of the van, threaded my way between the stored scenery and property baskets, rushed to the tailboard and threw up over it. At this point the van started to descend a hill, careering at about 40 miles an hour so that I was almost tipped out. My companions thought that I had flipped and was trying to commit suicide.

I have been sick in dressing-rooms, the wings, fire buckets, the backs of buses and in alleys behind the theatre. I did eventually summon up courage to see a doctor and the trouble was diagnosed as a duodenal ulcer. I have 'enjoyed' bad health ever since and have to be careful about my diet but I now have a 'magic' pill to take when trouble threatens so thankfully my throwing-up days are over.

In 1951 the Adelphi company got terribly adventurous and, in conjunction with CEMA of Northern Ireland, did a six week tour of the province with James Bridie's *Mr Gillie*, in which I played Mrs Gillie opposite Noel

Lloyd. We had taken the 14 foot high van across and its height and weight sometimes presented problems on the narrow, twisting Irish roads. One night, with blackness all around, we came to a bridge with high tension cables underneath its roof and a notice at its approach that said DANGER. The sides of the van were made of metal sheets, so danger there was indeed. One of the men climbed up the outside of the van until his head was level with the top. Hanging on precariously with one hand, a torch in the other, he guided the van very slowly, inch by inch, avoiding the cables, until it had fully cleared them and was safe on the other side. It had taken 20 minutes to travel those few yards, with at most only two inches to spare between van and cable. The rest of us broke into a relieved cheer when we were free to go on.

About half a mile down the road there was a signpost pointing out that our destination was back the way we had come. Somewhere along the way we had taken a wrong turning. So this time we got out of the van and the driver manoeuvred it round and back we went under the bridge, another hazardous clinging to the van, another 20 minutes lost. Then it began to rain . . .

One of the places we visited was Omagh. We discovered that the theatre was above the main hall with the usual number of steps to negotiate. But there was a sort of hoist at the side of the hall, chains and a net, so at least our things could be hauled up to stage level. I was responsible for the hamper which contained all the spotlights, cables and other electrical equipment, a heavy brute which I had packed carefully. The hoist was a bit rusty but the stage manager had managed to get it working. The props hamper and the costumes hamper had already successfully reached their destination. Two of us unloaded the electrics hamper from the van and put it in the net, slung it on to the hoist, and slowly it started to ascend. I turned back to the van to continue unloading when suddenly there was an urgent shout. 'Look out below!' I jumped back and the hamper, crashing down from a height of ten feet, just missed me, and smashed on to the ground. Oh God, I thought, there go all the lamps and the bulbs!

With great trepidation I lifted the lid of the hamper. Not a single bulb was broken, nor even cracked. So I was congratulated on my excellent packing, which was very gratifying, though I would like to have been congratulated also on my narrow escape from death.

During the tour we had Sundays off, and one Sunday a few of us went on a trip over the border from Enniskillen in the North into the Republic. When we arrived at the border post there was only a little old man in his Customs shed, blinking shortsightedly over his Sunday newspaper. We were not allowed to take the van across, so we left it near the old man's shed, alongside three or four empty coaches, and continued on foot, along a lane which eventually led into a small village called Black Lion. Northern Ireland was completely dry on Sundays and we had been told that we could get a drink in the village Post Office, as well as buy cigarettes, which were much cheaper in the Republic. A busload of people had preceded us to the border, and we had been some way behind the 30 or so people who had dismounted. When we turned a corner of the lane the village lay before us, completely deserted, not a soul in sight! We immediately thought of the *Marie Celeste* and other unsolved mysteries, but it was more important to find the Post Office than to speculate over missing bus passengers. We turned down a side street and found our objective, with shuttered windows and an air of dead respectability. 'Ever been had?' someone muttered.

One of us knocked on the door rather hesitantly. After a few moments it opened a crack and a creased face like a walnut appeared. We explained that so-and-so over the border had told us to call, and the door opened wider. 'Come in, come in, then, will you?' and the walnut beckoned us to follow him down a long narrow room. There was a counter near the door, which was the Post Office. The next counters were full of groceries and then at the end of the room came the bar, crammed with people, including the bus passengers who had disappeared so mysteriously, and other bus loads before them. There was also a policeman in his uniform, drinking deep from his glass of Guinness. We went to the bar and ordered our drinks. 'Sorry, ladies, but you'll have to sit in the parlour,' said the barman, and the four women in the party had to beat an ignominious retreat from the male territory and wait for their drinks to be brought to them in a room next door. It was a bit of a blow for 'ladies' who were the equals of the men in the company and did the same jobs, but we accepted our lower station in life with as much grace as we could muster for the sake of the nectar we were drinking.

During my second season with the Adelphis we did *Macbeth*, known during rehearsals as 'the Scottish play'. Its reputation for being an unlucky play if the real title is mentioned certainly held good for us. The culprit who had uttered the dread word 'Macbeth' in the dressing-room was never discovered, but he must have been responsible for the peculiar things that happened. The first was when Seumas Stewart, playing Macduff and the Bleeding Sergeant, sprained his wrist badly, which affected his swordplay. Then Wilfred Harrison, imported for the role of Macbeth, stepped off a high rostrum during a rehearsal, fell seven feet and was severely bruised.

But matters did not end there. I was playing First Witch, wearing a papier mâché mask with straggly hair attached, and gloves with long repulsive finger-nails sewn on the ends of the fingers. The mask had two eyeholes and a mouthhole and it all looked very weird. In the scene where Macbeth first confronts the witches we were standing on a rostrum which was just high enough to bring us on a level with Macbeth. In the half dark one night he began his speech, 'How, now, you secret, black and midnight hags – ' and spat right through the hole in my mask into my left eye.

I involuntarily closed my eye and found I could not open it again. A few seconds later he spat into my right eye! So I was totally blind and because of my long false finger-nails I could not wipe my eyes even if I could have poked a finger through the hole in the mask. I spent the rest of the scene with my eyes closed and then somehow fumbled my way offstage. I congratulated Wilfred on his excellent aim and in subsequent performances averted my face from him.

Our production of *Macbeth* involved a lot of scene changes which took place in blackouts. I was doubling the First Witch with Lady Macduff and had to change in the wings in the half dark. This particular stage, at Walkden near Manchester, had very little wing space and one of the flats was almost touching a banister rail on the front of the set, so that there were only about 18 inches of space to get through. As Macbeth made an exit I had to make an entrance carrying a stool which I was to be found sitting on when the lights came up. Macbeth came storming off with his cloak billowing behind him just as I was struggling to get on. We met and got jammed in the 18 inches space, Macbeth, cloak, stool and me. We pulled and pushed, twisted and turned, still in the dark, me getting panic-stricken in case I missed my entrance. Finally I fought my way past him and stumbled on to the stage, breathing heavily. I plonked my stool centre stage but before I could turn and sit on it the lights went up and the audience was treated to a marvellous view of Lady Macduff's backside. It received a round of applause from some irreverent spirits. *Macbeth* had struck again!

At Walkden the front curtain was enormously heavy and had to be wound up laboriously from the side of the stage; each half went up diagonally, and there were lots of chains sewn into the bottom to make it come down and hit the stage with a great crash. When we took the curtain call for *Macbeth*, for which the cast was unusually large and the stage small, the Lords in the play were set downstage on one knee and the rest of us were on various rostra behind them forming tableaux. This usually worked well, but not at Walkden. The men were wearing Viking-type helmets with horns on and John Slimming, one of the Lords, was very near the curtain when it swished down. The force of its descent knocked his helmet over his eyes and he fell flat on his face. He just managed to regain his kneeling position as the curtain went up for the second call. It descended, and John was again knocked over with his helmet askew. The rostra quivered with suppressed laughter. He righted himself, and it all happened again. He got up after the third call. 'I'm not bloody well putting up with this any longer!' he growled, and stormed off, his helmet dented, his horns bent and his feelings bruised. The rest of us took two more calls, shoulders heaving, and we wondered if the audience had noticed that there was a Lord missing.

We took the play to the old Hippodrome at Stockport. On the first night I took over the prompt corner with the text after the witches had vanished in the third scene. The fourth scene took place in a room of the palace at Forres. Firemen had been in to inspect the fireproofing arrangements, and some of them had stayed on to watch the show from the wings. One fireman was standing next to me. We had our own electric switchboard plugged into the main cable which came from the back of the stage across the wings. My fireman friend must have been standing on the cable, rocking backwards and forwards on his heels and, as his boots were steel-tipped, they wore through the insulation on the cable. Suddenly there was great bang and a big blue flash and the fireman was catapulted backwards with terrific force, hitting the wooden doors at the side. Naturally all the fuses went and the theatre was in total darkness.

Macbeth, Duncan, Malcolm and the rest, not knowing what had happened, struggled bravely with their lines, which got limper and limper as the brouhaha backstage grew noisier, and then the curtain came down. The stage manager went out front and told the audience what had happened and asked them to be patient while things were being put right – which took half an hour. And all this time the poor fireman was out cold. An ambulance arrived and he was taken to hospital. We heard later that he recovered and had only shock and bruises to show for his nasty experience; but I shivered for quite a long time afterwards. If I had been accidentally touching the fireman, even though I wasn't standing on the cable, I would have suffered the same fate. And we could both have been killed. An actor's life is as dangerous as a miner's, it seems to me, especially in *Macbeth*.

Next to *Macbeth* I think the most memorable production I did with the Adelphi was *Alice in Wonderland*. Seumas Stewart adapted it from the book and it was produced by Guy Vaesen, a brilliant young director with whom Noel Lloyd had worked at Great Yarmouth and had recommended to us. Guy was one of the most original and dynamic producers of the time, having been a protégé of Willard Stoker at the Liverpool Playhouse. He was such a stimulating person, very enthusiastic, very funny and he opened the eyes of the Adelphi to entirely new aspects of acting. He subsequently became a successful radio producer and, after retirement, an equally accomplished artist. Nowadays he lives on a Greek island and paints. Dear Guy, how much we learned from you!

Alice in Wonderland was a very colourful production, and was an absolute marathon, everybody playing two or three parts. I started off as an owl. Dressed in my home-made costume all I had to do was run around the stage, flap my wings and hoot – not a bit of heavy characterisation, I admit, but it was a funny little part. The Mock Turtle was played by that fine and versatile actor, Harry Towb, imported for the occasion by Guy, and my own cavortings in the Caucus Race made him fall about laughing. Each hoot I gave made him laugh a little bit more, so the proceedings were held up for a while. Fortunately, I did not get carried away and over-hoot so Harry was able to return to his mock-turtled lugubriousness and save the scene from utter collapse. I have a theory that all the best actors are great gigglers.

Laughing on stage is a strange phenomenon. I think it happens because of the heightened atmosphere, the knowledge that out there in the dark people are listening to your every word, and the constant effort to concentrate, and the slightest deviation from what has been planned and rehearsed can suddenly seem terribly funny. Even when a slip of the tongue or a wrong movement is not inherently risible the humorous potential cuts the tension and magnifies the absurdity of the situation. There are ways of containing the internal cauldron of laughter, but often it boils over and the actor is left helpless; and when the audience joins in there can be complete chaos.

I also played the Queen of Hearts in *Alice*, in a costume made of sacking which had been stiffened with size so that it could be flat at the sides to look like a playing card. Once I was in it I could hardly walk and certainly could not sit down. It had to be lowered over my head by two people who almost needed a crane. Dressing me was like a scene in *Henry V* when knights in armour were lowered on to their horses.

When I was not being an owl or a queen I was rushing off stage to take my turn on the prompt book or work the music. Music was a great feature of the production and there was a lot of it – on 78rpm records, the cues marked with a special kind of chalk, and one had to place the needle on *exactly* the right spot. The music used was Gordon Jacob's arrangement of Lecocq's *Mam'zelle Angot*, lovely, lively French ballet music which fitted the Alice songs with uncanny accuracy. *Alice in Wonderland* was a delight from start to finish. Guy had injected a new sense of fun and informality into a company which tended at times to be over-serious.

Guy stayed with the Adelphi company for their next production, Pinero's *Dandy Dick*, which gave him further scope for his daring and imaginative ideas. I played Salome, the dean's daughter, a comic little part which I enjoyed. The highlight was a sobbing match which I had with my sister in the play, though one local critic had the nerve to say that we 'over-sobbed'.

CHAPTER 8

Oldham Interlude

THE Adelphi company's unpaid summer break in 1950 lasted for two months, July and August. At the salary I was getting there was no way that I could afford to stay out of work for so long, and I thought I was lucky to get a special week with the Repertory Company in Bolton; that is, a week rehearsing and a week playing. What I did not reckon on was the fact that it was a twice nightly Rep. There are no such things these days, but thirty years ago twice nightly Rep was the norm – to be once nightly was heaven, and a play a fortnight was undreamed of luxury.

My week at Bolton almost destroyed my obsession with the theatre. After it was over I was almost ready to go back to the library. No, it wasn't quite as bad as that, nothing could be, but it was an awful experience, and all for £4 10s a week, providing your own clothes and paying for your own digs. And there were people who had been doing it for years and would do it all their working lives . . .

My memory has blanked out the name of the play but it must have been some potboiler where the plot was not affected if you left out half the dialogue. In any case the original play had been cut to ribbons. The schedule was punishing and the rehearsals slapdash.

We rehearsed in a top room of the pub next door to the theatre. People learned as many of their lines as they could and the rest they guessed or made up. We only had about two hours each morning to sketch out the play and stumble through the lines, and that was it. Moves, characterisation, motivation, were all stereotyped. By the opening on Monday night the play was still a shambles but we hoped that the worst of it was not going to show. We all flew around like scalded ferrets trying to remember what happened next, who came on and who went off. By the last performance on Saturday night it was certainly better but would not have pleased Sir Peter Hall. I suppose one's pride and integrity ensured improvement and a certain standard.

The first show started at a quarter to six and finished at half past seven, the audience being ushered out hurriedly so that the second house could begin at a quarter to eight. By a quarter to ten the theatre was empty. Between the shows it was impossible to relax; there was just time to change clothes, gulp a cup of tea and get to the wings for curtain up. Nor was there any respite during the intervals for they only lasted five minutes. And this went on six days a week. There were matinees on Thursday and Saturday – 14 shows altogether. Sunday was a day for sleeping, sorting out wardrobe and learning lines. That week at Bolton was the most hectic I have ever known and I swore that I would never play in twice nightly Rep again.

Back in Liverpool I had to sign on at the Labour Exchange. I turned down several jobs and was told that if I did not take the next one that was offered I would lose my dole money. The next one was as waitress in a holiday camp at Prestatyn. It did not sound too awful, so off I went. The camp may have been all that its owner had dreamed, and the campers were enjoying themselves, but behind the scenes it was dirty, chaotic and the staff quarters were squalid. I arrived in the middle of the day and was shown to a tatty little chalet where three other girls were sitting around, waiting for their afternoon shift. They were in various stages of undress, smoking, and telling stories that I, though no prude, did not like. Then I was taken to the kitchen, given a rather greasy uniform and shown how to serve afternoon teas. The kitchen was, well, not clean, the noise was deafening and the smell stomach-turning. Somehow I managed to get through the next couple of hours and actually delivered tea and cakes to the right people at the right tables. After the tea session I marched back to my chalet, picked up my bag which I had not begun to unpack, and found the office. 'I'm sorry, I'm not staying,' I told the lady behind the desk.

'I didn't think you'd last long,' she said, looking me up and down, 'but I didn't think it would be as brief as this.' I collected half a day's pay and returned home, where I stayed until it was time to go back to Macclesfield.

In the spring of 1951 The Adelphi Guild Theatre came to an end. The cause was not lack of commitment or enthusiasm; it was that the company had come to the end of its resources. An autumn tour had been booked and for the first time an Arts Council grant had been promised, but there was a gap of three months or so when financial commitments far outweighed the income. So, sorrowfully, the Adelphi company disbanded.

I think I was the only member who continued with an acting career. Noel Lloyd had already left and was with the Southport Rep. The others returned to real life and devoted their skills to various activities unconnected with the theatre. It was the end of an era, and I was moved too, though not as much as those who had given so much of their time and talents to make their ideals live. The difference between them and me was that they were at heart amateurs, in the best sense of the word, while I set out to be a true professional. Their standards were high and in practical matters they were superb, but they did love to talk, to smoke pipes and look solemn, to worry topics like a dog with a bone, to discuss abstract ideas, to move on a higher plane than mere mortals like me who just wanted to get on with the job. I, devoted to the theatre, determined to learn my craft to the best of my ability, was much less concerned with philosophy, and I was not a natural vagabond.

It was not selfishness that led me down a different path. It was a different outlook on the realities and values of the profession. I was very fond of my fellow Adelphi members and I think they were of me; we had lots of fun together and I certainly pulled my weight both on the stage and behind the scenes. But I was not as devastated as the others were when the venture failed. For me it was a curtain coming down on a scene, not the end of the play. It was a time, not to look back, but to plunge ahead with banners unfurled.

I wrote to Guy Vaesen who was by now the resident director of the Oldham Rep (once nightly and of a high standard!) and asked if there was any chance of working with him. But it was halfway through the season, his company was complete, and all he could offer me was a job as wardrobe mistress and an occasional part when he could fit me in. It did not sound very exciting, but it was better than a series of holiday camps. Then, too, I could sew . . .

On the whole Oldham was not a good experience, even though I enjoyed being with Guy again, and I only stayed for four months, during which time I played in *I Killed the Count*, by Alec Coppel, and in *Dandy Dick* again. I had the same part as in Guy's previous production, and I met Bernard Cribbins, who also appeared in it. What I remember chiefly about my sojourn in Oldham was my digs, and that memory is etched on my mind for ever.

The day I arrived in Oldham was unseasonably hot and I had to walk from the station to the theatre carrying all my worldly possessions in two heavy suitcases. The stage manager gave me an address where I might find a room and I heaved myself and cases halfway across Oldham again and eventually found the house I was looking for. It was in a side street, a tall narrow house wedged between a pub and what looked like a small engineering works. I knocked and the door was opened by an elderly lady about five feet tall and just as wide. She was round-faced, red-cheeked and her hair was short, white and curly. She seemed to fill the hall she stood in; it was about the size of a hearth rug and the stairs went straight up from it.

'Come in, love,' she said when I had explained who I was. 'Yes, I've got a room. Come into my sitting-room and we'll talk things over.'

Her sitting-room was to the right of the front door and was crammed with furniture – tables, chairs, dressers, whatnots, knick-knacks by the dozen, and a bed behind the door. I could not imagine how she got around in it; it took me all my time to manoeuvre myself into a chair. 'As this is my daughter's house,' she announced, 'I'll have to charge you 25 shillings a week. But I'll throw in a pint of milk a day.' Milk cost about 4½d. a pint so it really was a bonus. My salary was to be £5, no advance on the Adelphi rate. After a little more chat she led the way up the steep steps from the minute hall, she rolling from side to side and panting heavily, and me wondering what would happen if she fell backwards.

There was a door at the top of the stairs and she squeezed herself through. 'Now this is your kitchen and bathroom,' she said. She indicated a rickety old table on which stood a galvanised metal food safe, black with age. Across the room was what must have been the oldest gas stove out of a museum, blue and mottled and encrusted with the remains of a thousand meals. I discovered later that only one of the rings worked. When I applied a match the flame would shoot up about 18 inches then subside to less that half an inch and it was impossible to regulate. A kettle took half an hour to boil. One day I went to open the oven door, lifted the latch and the whole door fell off and landed on my foot – there were no pins in the hinges. Neither were there any shelves, burners nor bottom to it. So bang went any ideas of cooking a Sunday roast.

As a contrast there was, on the other side of the room, a new and shining porcelain bath and wash basin to match, looking incongruous in their surroundings. An old wooden mangle stood under the window. The loo was in a small area partitioned off with hardboard and had a very warped door. Inside was a high cistern with a long chain. I soon discovered just what hazards were involved in going to the loo. When I pulled the chain I had to dash for the exit, but as the door stuck it was several seconds before I could yank it open. In that space of time half the contents of the cistern had gone down the lavatory pan, the rest came over the top of the cistern and drowned me. Every time, without fail. So I evolved a plan. I got the door open first, then pulled the chain and ran like hell to the other side of the kitchen – and then had to mop up the overflow. It was as dramatic a performance as ever I gave on the stage.

My landlady pointed out a big cupboard with no doors in which sat the biggest copper tank I have ever seen, over five feet high. 'Now, love,' she said, 'there's always hot water, so you can have a bath any time you like.' I could hardly believe my ears. In theatrical digs one was usually allocated a certain time on a certain evening and if you missed it there was no chance of a bath until the following week.

'I go to wash up at my daughter's pub every night,' the old lady went on, 'but before I go out at nine o'clock I'll put the immersion heater on.'

After my first evening at the theatre I did not get back to the house until about eleven o'clock. As I put the key in the lock I heard a bumping noise – a sort of vibratory booming. It must be coming from next door, I thought, the engineering or printing works doing overtime. But when I opened the door the vibration was more severe and the noise louder; in fact, the entire house was shaking. It was all very puzzling, but having a bath was uppermost in my mind so I hurried to the bathroom-cum-kitchen. The tank in the cupboard was literally rocking from side to side and a furious bubbling noise was coming from the interior like an over-excited witches' cauldron rocking in its moorings. Intrepid as ever, I rushed across to it, switched off the heater then turned on the bath tap, from which pure scalding steam hissed out and filled the room with what looked like old-fashioned London fog. I opened the window and fled up to my bedroom on the next floor. After about ten minutes I dared to creep down and found, to my relief, that real water was running into the bath.

After that I hurried away from the theatre at curtain down every night, never staying for a drink or a chat, and ran all the way to my digs in order to switch the heater off before the whole thing exploded. The trouble was, I found out, that there was no thermostat, so for two hours the water had been getting hotter and hotter. I was a bit diffident in those days and did not like to tell the landlady in case she took umbrage and refused to provide any hot water at all, so making me forfeit my precious baths!

My bedroom was numbingly cold. It had a standing black stove and my landlady would leave paper and wood chips in it, but I never dared to light it in case it behaved in an aggressive way like the boiler. So I would get into bed quickly. The sheets were coarse but clean, the mattress and pillow were filled with straw. On my first night I thought the rustling might have been something that was not me moving in the bed . . .

The bedroom also contained a big overstuffed armchair, which I thought was covered with grey velvet until I happened to put my hand on it and found that if it had not been so thick with dust the grey would have been green.

All these things were not calculated to make me feel at ease, but things finally came to a head when I realised why the wall of an alcove in the corner where I hung my clothes on pegs was pasted over with brown paper. Having lived in Liverpool and knowing a bit about housing conditions (though not, I emphasise, in No. 18, Rhiwlas Street!) brown paper meant bugs. The theory was that they could not get through, but I wasn't going to give them a chance. After a fortnight I told the old lady that I was going to leave her.

She cried and begged me to stay! She liked having me there although we rarely saw each other, and for a moment my tender heart nearly persuaded me to rescind my notice. Then I thought of the loo and the heater and the cooker and the armchair and the bugs and the general discomfort and I muttered something about having to find digs nearer the theatre, feeling mean and courageous at the same time. I'm sure that area of Oldham must have been pulled down long ago, though I would not be surprised if one house had blown up long before it could be bull-dozed.

My job at Oldham as wardrobe mistress was very time-consuming. We seemed to do a lot of costume plays, the clothes for which were hired from a theatrical costumier's in Manchester, and of course they had to be altered to fit the contours of the actors. The costumes would arrive on Saturday and I took the alteration measurements when and how I could on that day. On Sunday I went to the theatre to get the work done. We were preparing for *The Knight of the Burning Pestle* and I knew I was going to have to work a very long day, a prospect that filled me with some foreboding, because it meant that I would be alone in the theatre for hours, and I hated the thought. An empty theatre backstage is always spooky; I suppose it's because the ghosts of long dead actors are never very far away, invisible but still mumbling their lines and savouring their triumphs. I found myself looking over my shoulder for no good reason, not seeing nor hearing anything but somehow conscious that there was an atmosphere, a heightened tension, even a feeling of expectancy. As I am completely sceptical about ghosts and the paranormal I could, on reflection, shrug such fancies away, but still I was never at ease in the silence.

The scenic artist came in later that Sunday to work on his set and I was glad to see him. He was on the stage and I was in the long dressing-room used by all the girls, and we both got on happily with our respective jobs for a couple of hours or so. Then he came up and said, 'Look, Jean, I've got to go home to collect some brushes I left behind. I'll only be about 20 minutes, will you be all right on your own?'

'Yes,' I said, but a little hesitantly for it was dark now and there were shadows in the corners and ghostly costumes hanging up on rails looking like actors preparing to go on stage. However, he went and I continued to sew. Simple costume accessories like gloves were not hired and there were some big skips at the far end of the dressing-room which I knew contained a mass of oddments accumulated over the years. I opened the first skip, took out an armful of bits and pieces, dumped it on the floor, plunged my hands in again to take out another bundle – and the bundle moved before I could touch it. Then out jumped a rat, a huge gingery creature that landed on the floor with a thud and crouched there, looking at me. I slammed down the lid of the basket, fought back a scream and retreated to my chair and climbed on to it. The rat continued to look at me. Then, 'Hell!' I thought, 'I'm not going to have my work interrupted by a mere *rat*,' and I sat down, legs tucked under me, and got on with my sewing, though the stitches were not as even as they should have been.

The rat, tired of the view, began to run about. He leapt on to one of the dressing-tables and nibbled at a stick of greasepaint. The taste evidently pleased him and he carried on, first a stick of Leichner No 5, then No 9. Then the rat inched nearer to the table at which I was working and eyed me brazenly. My courage, always brittle in such situations, suddenly gave way and I acknowledged that the rat had won. I gathered up my sewing and fled down to the open stage door in the alley, and continued to work by the lamp over the door, feeling pretty silly.

The scenic artist returned and stared at me. 'What on earth are you doing out here?' he asked.

'There's a rat in the dressing-room,' I said.

'Not for long, there isn't,' he declared and went into the theatre. A couple of minutes later I heard running footsteps and a great shooshing and the red-eyed monster scuttled down the alley.

'Thank you,' I said tremulously.

Back in the dressing-room I refused to go near the skip in case there were any members of the rat's family lying doggo in their squat. Luckily all the things I wanted I found elsewhere.

Here I want to mention John Barrie, who later altered the whole course of my life. The first week I was at Oldham they were doing *Top of the Ladder* and John was playing the lead, but as he left the company at the end of that first week I really did not get to know him well. Years later, when I left Southport and went to York, it was his last week there when it was my first. So, although we became friends, we did not work together. It was he who was responsible for my entry into the TV world. John is dead now. He was a fine actor and some of his performances at Oldham, in *Death of a Salesman* and *Harvey*, for instance, were masterly. He later became well-known for his role of Sergeant Cork in the TV police series.

After four months in Oldham I decided that I was not getting enough acting experience and I left, with no hard feelings between Guy and me. He understood how I felt and I knew that he could do no more for me than he was doing. I returned to Liverpool, rather depressed at my lack of prospects and also because I would not be going back to my old home in Arnold Street, but to my aunt Lal, my father's sister, in Enid Street, who had agreed to put me up for a short time.

CHAPTER 9

Another New Beginning

A YEAR before, while I was still with the Adelphi company, my father had been made redundant. After working for the same company for 37 years he had received a minute's notice. He had been working on the *Himalaya* which was built in Barrow, and had gone on trials with the ship. The trials finished at Southampton and dad immediately returned to Liverpool. The next day he went to work expecting to be allocated another job. Instead, he was greeted with, 'Sorry, Archie, the firm is being reorganised and there's no job for you. Sorry, mate, but you're out.'

Dad could hardly believe his ears. They told him that his particular job was to go in the reorganisation and no one else was being appointed. No, it was not his work that was at fault.

He was offered a job as an electrician, but not as a foreman electrician that he had been before going to Barrow – someone else had that job and it couldn't be taken from him. As that someone was a man my father had trained it would have meant working under him. 'No, thank you,' dad said, and he left. All he got apart from the wages due was an illuminated address testifying to his conscientiousness; of a golden handshake not a penny. Dad was devastated that his loyalty to the firm and devotion to his work had counted for nothing. 'After 37 years,' he said bitterly, and it was a long time before he became reconciled to the situation.

He tried for job after job, but without any success. He was too old at 57 and he was resigning himself to spending the rest of his working life on the dole when, through a friend of my mother's, they were offered a joint position as caretakers of a Baptist Theological College in Manchester.

Reluctantly they sold the Arnold Street house and moved to strange surroundings in a strange town. The college was enormous; they had all the cleaning and minor maintenance to do, and also helped the students in various ways. It was hard, exhausting work, and they did it for £5 a week between them. The sum included rent, rates and meals, of course, but even so it was not over-generous. By this time Ken and his family had a house in Sale, near Altrincham, and took some of the furniture from Arnold Street. Mum and dad's tiny flat at the top of the college building could accommodate very little so the rest of the furniture had to be sold.

They endured this existence for five years and grew more and more unhappy. For the first time ever they began to snap at each other, even had proper rows. I think it was all due to a feeling of impermanence and their complete exhaustion. I was very worried about the situation but did not know what to do. Once or twice they were able to put me up for a weekend but I never enjoyed myself. It was very hard seeing my dear mum and dad so much on edge, but a solution to the problem did not present itself for a long time.

So I was staying with my aunt and wondering how long I would be able to endure an existence that was stale and unprofitable when I received a telegram from a man called Donald Bodley who ran the Rep at Southport, just up the coast from Liverpool. Southport was supposed to be a 'posh' town, the home of a lot of wealthy, elderly residents, and had the famous Lord Street running through it; oh, and the sea hardly ever came in, or it went out so far that nobody ever saw it. I knew it from day trips as a child. The telegram asked me if I would like to go over for an interview for a special week; my name had been given to him by a former colleague of mine. Well, a special week (shades of Bolton) was better than nothing and Laurence Olivier *might* be sitting in the audience one night, so I shot up to Southport.

I found when I got there that the person who had recommended me was Noel Lloyd, once with me in the Adelphi, and now a permanent member of the Southport company. I was offered the part of Ida in *See How They Run* and accepted it gladly. I loved the part; the character is a real scene-stealer. *See How They Run* must be one of the funniest farces ever written, based on the notion that if one vicar is funny a whole clutch of vicars is even funnier, and with a bishop added it becomes a riot.

A new assistant stage-manager joined the company on the first night, one not accustomed to the routine of telling the actors that the curtain was about to go up. During the interval after the first act three of the vicars were lounging about on the stage, I was waiting at the bottom of the stairs to get off, and the actress playing Miss Skillon, the obligatory middle-aged spinster, having fainted at the end of the first act, was sitting up chatting animatedly to the bishop. With no warning the curtain suddenly rose. Miss Skillon gave a startled 'Oh!' and flopped back into her faint. The rest of us fled, fighting to get offstage through the fireplace, out of the french windows, up the stairs, any way we could. The audience was stunned and did a collective double take.

In spite of this contretemps the play was a huge success and Donald was pleased with my performance. He asked me to stay on for another week, then another, and another, and after seven *years* I said, 'Donald, that's enough! It's the longest special week in the history of the theatre!' and I left.

Mrs Booth, my landlady in Southport, was a delightful lady but very talkative. She and Mr Booth had been married for a very long time and he had got used to her constant chattering. He would sit behind his newspaper and just grunt now and again. This was not much fun for her so when I came in late after the show she transferred her attentions to me. She knew I had to learn lines for the next day's rehearsal and did not mean to put me off but she was constitutionally incapable of being silent. While I was sipping my cocoa, the play open on my knee, she would start . . .

'Now I know I mustn't interrupt you but before you start I must tell you about Mrs Ecclestone down the road and what happened when she took her coat to be cleaned – at Burke's, you know, the one next to the greengrocer where Edie Sumner lost her purse in the brussels sprouts the time when Nora Evans was helping out – last November it must have been – no, I tell a lie, it was earlier because Albert had just been told about his grumbling appendix . . .' And she would go on and on. Meanwhile, I would be learning my lines, the monotone going into one ear and out of the other. This was the reason why I became able to learn lines when there was noise all around me. Now I can't learn at all unless there *is* noise. A radio, a conversation, a typewriter tapping, the wheels of a train rumbling, and words just seep into my mind and stay there. I feel like Susan Leg in E.F. Benson's *Secret Lives*, who could not compose her deathless prose until the loudest possible music filled her ears. Mrs Booth never expected me to talk back at her. An occasional 'Fancy that!', 'You don't say!' or a simple 'Yes' would satisfy her.

Mrs Booth's daughter and her husband, Andy Grosart, lived upstairs, and when I heard the unusual name I said to him, 'My uncle Bill in Liverpool had a friend of the same name over 20 years ago.'

'That must have been my eldest brother,' said Andy. So here I was living in the same house as the brother of the man who had sung duets with my uncle Bill in my grandparents' cellar all those years ago. We all agreed that it's a funny old world. Both the Booths are dead now, though Mr Booth reached his hundredth birthday. They were a kindly couple, he as reticent as she was voluble, and I kept up with them for many years. I still see Andy Grosart and his wife.

CHAPTER 10

All Work and More Plays

I WENT to Southport in September, 1951 and left in August, 1958. Not counting weeks when I was not cast in a play (very rarely), holidays and two weeks of pantomime every year, I calculate that I must have done nearly 300 plays: comedy, drama, farce, tragedy, romantic costume, detective (oh, those *awful* Agatha Christies!), classics – I can't think of a type I have not done. And when I add the plays I later did at York the total was almost 400. There must be actors who have exceeded that total, but I think I come pretty high up in the league table.

In Southport we played in the Little Theatre. It belonged to the amateurs who, for one winter season, needed it temporarily for one of their own productions, so we retired to a theatre called the Casino on the promenade at the beginning of the pier. It was made of wood and must have been the biggest fire risk in the whole of Southport. The two dressing-rooms were above the stage level on the first floor; stairs led to them from either side of the stage, one set for the men and the other for the women. The tongue and groove boards of the walls had warped so much that in places there were two inch gaps and we could see Blackpool Tower through the holes. When it rained in a certain direction we got the full blast and our clothes got drenched. And we had rats . . . They used to crawl up the piles of the pier from the water and make straight for the theatre. Like my rat at Oldham his Southport cousins liked greasepaint and any left out on a dressing-table would be found chewed up next day. We once raised the curtain for rehearsal and found its bottom fringe lying on the floor. The rats had eaten it off.

Another hazard was the wind. Any seaside resort in winter is among the coldest places in the country, and as we were only at the Casino in winter we were subject to positive gales. The prevailing wind was westerly and the stage door faced the sea, and we had to go into the theatre as a bunch because one person on his own could not open the stage door against the wind.

I really hated the winters in Southport. I've been blown back many a time whilst trying to walk along the promenade and sometimes we could not even cross the road. We always prepared a couple of hot water bottles and whoever was off stage would hug one of them fiercely and then pass it on to someone else when he or she had to make an entrance. The Casino audience would also bring rugs and hot water bottles with them. There weren't an awful lot of them, except on Fridays and Saturdays, but I must say they were a faithful lot!

At the Casino, oddly enough, we always seemed to be doing plays in which the women wore low-cut evening dresses or swim suits. You could not really hug a hot water bottle on stage when you were supposed to be on the Riviera so we shivered and went blue and longed for the summer and an end to the dreaded Casino.

It was there that I lost another of my nine lives when the fire curtain was due to be lowered, as it had to be when there was no audience, though nobody thought for a moment that it would be of any use, up or down, if anyone put a match to the wooden tinderbox. This particular fire curtain was hand-cranked and when raised it was like a huge sword of Damocles hanging over our heads. The stage manager had gone to operate the curtain, perhaps not feeling as strong as he usually did, and his grasp of the wheel as the curtain slowly descended was not as firm. I was downstage near the footlights making notes on my script when there was a shout from above the stage. 'Look out below!' Shades of the hoist at Omagh! I heard a rumbling and saw the curtain falling down – on me . . . I literally dived off the stage into the auditorium, luckily not breaking anything, but I felt the wind of the curtain coming down as it missed me by inches and crashed on to the stage, breaking several boards. At the 'inquest' later it turned out that a couple of the cogs on the wheel had broken and the stage manager just could not hold it. I kept well away from the line of descent in future.

*

Before we had to spend our winter in the Casino I was in my first pantomime at the Little Theatre in the 1951 Christmas season: *The Sleeping Beauty*, I think it was. One of my parts was that of the front end of the horse and Stanley Lloyd, the stage manager, was the back end. We had to arrange and practise little dances for the horse and our enthusiasm was such that we were discovered in Lord Street one day practising our dance, Stanley behind me with his hands round my waist and our legs going out sideways, not always in unison. I expect the good people of Southport were only confirmed in their belief that actors were mad.

My horse part caused me a great deal of anguish in one way or another. The costume consisted of two pairs of felt trousers with black hooves stitched on the bottoms of the legs and elastic to go under the feet. The head was attached to the body and inside it was a device that fitted over my own head, so that my face was really in the horse's neck. If anyone touched the head the sound echoed inside the hollow space and it was rather like being thumped with a sledge-hammer. There was a tiny gauze eyehole in the neck and through it I could just about see the floor. My back half, of course, could not see anything.

The trousers must have been made for giants. They were all right for Stanley, because he was tall, but the waist of my trousers came up under my arms and I had to tie them round the middle with a piece of rope. One night, during the horse dance, I felt the rope go slack and the trousers begin to slip down. 'Stan,' I whispered, 'help, my trousers are falling down.'

'Right,' he said, 'the next time you jump I'll lift them up.' So he grabbed the trousers, which were by that time on my backside and going up and down like Norah Batty's stockings. I leapt up about four feet but Stan did not realise how light I was. He hoisted me up by the trousers, then lost his balance and sat down with a thud. I came to earth and sat down too – on the recumbent Stanley. By this time we were laughing so much that we could not get up again for ages. It was worse for Stan than it was for me because he could not see a thing and he had to rely on me to guide him. The dance remained unfinished and we shuffled off the stage and collapsed in another heap in the wings.

At one point in each performance the horse would cautiously creep down the steps into the auditorium and give a ride to one or two of the children. They would clamber into the gangway and pat my head – my real head ringing like church-bells: some would poke us with busy little fingers and we would hear, 'It's only people inside . . .' Sometimes we were kicked and punched so mercilessly that suddenly I would say to Stan, 'That's enough. We'll gallop to the top of the gangway, turn round and then straight back to the stage, we're not putting up with any more of that!' So we would clear the floor and set off at a gallop, scattering the children right and left. Once we nearly trod on a baby who had crawled out into the gangway. I spotted it just in time and yelled, 'Brakes on, Stan!' and we skidded to a stop like something in a Keystone Cops comedy, not quite flattening the child. But it was a near thing.

That was the only time I played half a horse, but as Donald Bodley always liked to have animals in his pantomimes I have been three different kinds of cats, a panda and Mother Bear, and each time I had to make my own costume. When I played the panda I made the head and body out of a blanket, but I had to do something about the arms and legs, which had to be black. So I took the costume home the night before the dress rehearsal to dye them. I did the dyeing in the sink and hung the costume on a coat hanger to let it drip. As the dye came out in purple streams the sink and surrounding bit of the kitchen was an exotic sight. In the morning the arms and legs were still wet and I had to take the costume to the theatre as it was. I put it in the boiler room for a time, then tried a hair dryer on it, but nothing was successful and when I put it on the panda still had wet limbs. The rehearsal lasted from 10.30 a.m. until 11 p.m. and when I finally took the costume off my arms and legs were a real bright purple and remained so for the duration of the run. No amount of scrubbing would restore me to a normal skin colour and I received some peculiar looks, in and around the theatre.

The panda used to go down to the audience with a little basket of sweets which it would distribute to children sitting in the gangway seats. One night I gave a sweet to a little round-eyed boy who was having a wonderful time. On my journey back to the stage his little hand shot out and grabbed my paw. 'I've had one of your sweets,' he said, 'now you must have one of mine,' and he put an unwrapped piece of sticky toffee into my paw and closed my real hand round it.

'Thank you,' I mumbled and hurried back on stage to do my funny song and bring the scene to an end. In the wings I found that I could not unclose my paw; the heat and stickiness had caused the toffee to turn into superglue and it had stuck firmly to the blanket. It was a very nasty mess, and I swore in future never to take sweets from a stranger!

In *The Sleeping Beauty* not only did I play the horse but also a village maiden in the first scene. My job was to rush on stage with the news that the baby was born, and all the other villagers were supposed to receive the news with exclamations of delight. My shoes had leather soles which had got slippery with use and once when I dashed on my foot slipped and I took a header straight for the footlights. I had a sudden vision of going headlong into the orchestra pit so I put out my hands to stop myself. They came to rest in the footlights, which were covered with red and blue gelatines and fixed to a metal bar. The lamps had been burning for some time and when my hands touched them the gelatines melted on to the lamps and covered my hands with red and blue. The audience broke into applause, thinking I had done something brilliantly rehearsed, and behind me the actors quivered with suppressed laughter, convinced that it was the funniest bit of spontaneous business they had ever seen.

I jumped up, grinning like a country bumpkin, announced the arrival of the baby, and tried to pretend that my hands were not terribly blistered. 'That was very funny, Jean,' Donald Bodley said after the show. 'Do you think you could keep it in?'

'Have you seen my hands?' I snarled, holding them out.

The old saying that an actor should never act with children or animals can be true; in our case not with animals and, when we were doing *Cinderella*, particularly not with rabbits. For one of the woodland scenes Donald had decided that real rabbits on the stage would provide a pretty touch to the serenading of Cinderella by Prince Charming while she was sitting on a log and looking pensive. So we borrowed half a dozen rabbits from a local pet shop and kept them in hutches below stage until they were needed, well supplied with lettuce and carrots. On the first night the creatures tried to eat the grass painted on the backcloth, and when they found that it was not a very productive pastime they got a bit nasty. We did not realise that we had a mixed bunch of bucks and does, but they seemed to know the difference and proceeded to enjoy that difference all over the stage. Most of the children did not know what was going on but their parents did and reacted accordingly. The stage manager tried to tempt the rabbits off stage with carrots but they were having too good a time on stage and refused to leave.

In the meantime Cinderella was getting restive. Then in came the prince who put one foot on the log and began to sing. The young man was not really a very good singer, but in Rep everybody sometimes has to do things at which they are not expert, and he was doing his best. Suddenly he was aware of little sniggers from the audience, then outright titters, finally a great belly-laugh. He was furious, convinced that they were laughing at him and his vocal inadequacy: what he did not know was that the biggest rabbit had stationed himself behind the log and every time the prince reached a higher and less melodious note two rabbit ears would appear above the log, as though on cue, then a rabbit face; there would be a couple of twitches of the rabbit nose and then the head would disappear. This happened several times and the audience was rocking with laughter. So was Cinderella. She could see what was happening but was unable to warn the prince of the opposition, and he stormed off stage at the end of his song – to huge applause. Being a good-natured young man he soon regained his composure though he swore that if those rabbits did not disappear, he would. Donald saw the point, and the rabbits' brief hour of glory came to an end.

On the second night he provided four geese instead! Without any rehearsal the birds took over as the rabbits had done, but in a different way. They ran around being frightfully aggressive, nipping the ankles of anybody who came within range of their beaks. Cinderella tucked her feet under her and the prince had to shift from foot to foot, slyly kicking out to right and left while in midsong. Then two of the geese decided to join the audience and nipped the ankles of the people in the front row of the stalls, causing not a little pandemonium. A stagehand caught them and took them away and the pantomime went on without benefit of bird or beast. After that Donald saw the light, at least for the run of that pantomime.

Another Christmas play caused an incident in which I was painfully involved. The play was Eleanor Farjeon's *The Silver Curlew*, a charming play with music. I played the heroine's nanny and at one point had to be carried on stage by the prince, piggy-back style. He was tall and I was short, so to get on his back I stood on a couple of steps in the wings and leapt into position. There was a thunder sheet hanging from the flies, and although it was not required for this particular play some foolish person had lowered it so that it hung just above the prince's head. Being semi-dark in the wings neither of us noticed this large sheet of metal hanging from two ropes. I got on my two steps, jumped off on to the prince's back, and cracked my head on the heavy metal. On stage it was a beautiful summer afternoon with not a cloud in the sky: an idyll that was rudely shattered by a tremendous crack of thunder . . . In the wings one dazed nanny prepared to make an entrance not knowing where she was or what had happened to her. The intrusive sound had also dazed the actors and the scene was played by all in a state of bewilderment.

In May, 1953 we thankfully gave the Little Theatre back to the amateurs, and left the Casino to rot away quietly, while we took over the Scala, once a theatre, then a cinema, now a theatre again. It looked like a theatre, felt like one, and we were happy there; and the audiences grew bigger every week. At last the town became really aware of our existence. Gadgets worked properly, dressing-rooms were dry, not a rat was seen. Things will stop happening to me at last, I thought, but I was wrong . . .

Roseanne, one of the girls in the company, was the daughter of the owner of the Brunswick Hotel at the end of Lord Street. When she got married we were all invited to the wedding and to the reception afterwards at the hotel. Being a Saturday we had two shows to do. We finished rehearsal early and met at our local pub near the theatre to drink the bride's health while we were waiting for taxis to take us to the church. In those 20 minutes I consumed three Guinnesses, goodness knows why. At the reception there were waiters going around with trays of drinks and dishes of delicious things to nibble. As actors are never averse to free food and drink we tucked into whatever was being offered, including the drinks. At two o'clock lunch was announced! We had not expected this at all but we sat down to a splendid lunch accompanied by fine wines, followed by champagne for the toasts.

By this time it was past four o'clock and we had to be in the theatre at half past four for the first call. Stanley Lloyd and I opened the play so it was urgent that we should leave quickly. We ran all the way to the theatre, the wine inside us getting very agitated. I remember sitting in the dressing-room trying to put my make-up on, and failing even to see my face in the mirror. It was one of the two times in my life that I have been drunk, either on or off stage (not counting the episode of the port in grandma's cellar), and I did not enjoy the experience.

The play was a north country comedy whose name I have forgotten. I was discovered standing at the ironing board and I did not even know in which direction the audience was, and when I spoke I did not know what words I was saying. They came out very faint and faraway but without any slurring. Inside I was hissing, 'Come on! Pull yourself together!' In the interval I said to the girl on the prompt book, 'Do I seem to be faint this afternoon?'

'Jean,' she said, 'You're shouting twice as loud as you usually do!'

Stan and I drank black coffee in the interval and in between the shows and in the middle of the first act of the second performance we both became sober; it was just as if a hypnotist had snapped his fingers and ordered the effects of the drink to disappear. And I thought, 'Thank God, I know what I'm doing at last . . .' I had learned my lesson. I never drank before a show again, nor during a performance, and only very moderately after a show.

Stanley Lloyd, my stage manager friend, had a phobia about spiders; he would turn green if even the smallest, most harmless specimen crossed his path. At the Scala we were doing a play about a young couple who had just returned from a holiday abroad, all tanned and gorgeous, and who were recounting their experiences to the rest of us on stage. I think I was playing a mother (a not unusual bit of casting). Stan was sitting in an armchair and doing most of the talking. I was on a sofa next to his 'wife' – who suddenly muttered out of the corner of her mouth, 'Look over there . . .' Now I am rather short-sighted and the stage was quite a wide one, but I could see, stumping out of the opposite wings towards Stan's chair, the biggest spider I have ever seen, fully two inches across the body and with long hairy legs. It was like a walking ball of black wool. Those of us who had seen it were riveted, hypnotised by this tarantula-like creature and the way it was making directly towards Stan – and wondering what he would do when he saw it.

Suddenly he did! He went mottled under his Mediterranean tan, and a terrified grimace appeared on his face. He lifted his feet from the floor and remained sitting with his legs hovering in mid-air; and all the time he went on talking, not missing a line or a cue; a wonderful example of bravery in the face of overwhelming odds. The spider crawled past him and came to rest near the sofa on which I was sitting. All eyes were on it although our mouths were uttering the frivolous lines of the play. Then it put a spurt on and hurried across to the fireplace. I took my eyes off it for a moment, but when I looked back it had disappeared. My next move was towards the actor who was playing the father. He was standing with one shoe half off his foot. 'Where did it go?' I said under my breath and in his best ventriloquial voice he answered, 'Into the fireplace – I was going to hit it with my shoe but it was too quick for me.' Then he spoke the line that brought the curtain down at the end of the act.

We all rushed into the wings – all except Stan, who remained rooted to his armchair. The prompter was standing on his stool, trousers rolled up, face like a piece of parchment. 'It ran up the curtains,' he quavered.

And there the spider stayed. When we took our curtain calls we stood as far away from the footlights as possible and the audience must have thought we were a very bashful lot. Our eyes followed the curtain as it went up and down, but the monster failed to appear, and we never saw it again. I presume it stayed aloft for the rest of its life, as frightened of us as we were of it.

The worst and most inexcusable attack of outright laughter that both cast and audience joined in was when we were doing a farce by Philip King and Anthony Armstrong called *Here We Come Gathering*. A young married couple and their in-laws go to view a country cottage separated from the mainland by a stream and reached only by a wooden bridge. A storm arises, the stream bursts its banks, the bridge is swept away and the party is marooned. There is no food in the cottage. Their eventual rescuer is Evadne Potter, a Girl Guide, who swings like Tarzan across the stream from a tree. All she can offer the people to eat are jelly babies which she brings out in a paper bag from the leg of her knickers.

Evadne Potter was played by Elizabeth McKenzie, who was tall and slim, dressed in a schoolgirl's gymslip, doing a perfect Joyce Grenfell. Very solemnly Evadne offered the bag to the young husband, played by Stanley Lloyd, and as he took one she said, in a dreadfully chummy way, 'What colour have you got? Oh, blackcurrant – yes, they're the ones I always suck a bit before I put them back . . .'

At that point, and it was due entirely to the way that Elizabeth delivered the line, we all collapsed – except for Stan. He was furious because he had the next line that brought down the curtain and he could not get it out. His fury grew the more we laughed, sitting on the floor with reddening faces and heaving shoulders, making no effort to hide our mirth. The play simply went to pieces, and the audience, seeing the state we were in, joined in, instead of getting indignant and demanding their money back, as they had every right to do. The theatre rang with spontaneous laughter. Once we almost composed ourselves and were about to carry on but a guffaw from the front row set us off again. This went on for what seemed like several minutes but could not have been more than two. In the wings Donald was pacing up and down, mouthing what we assumed were mighty oaths; and this caused a further outbreak.

Finally, out of sheer exhaustion, we straightened our faces and concentrated on Stan, still fuming away quietly, waiting to speak his long delayed line. He opened his mouth – and out came the biggest laugh of the evening so far. From then on it was chaos on both sides of the footlights. The stage manager rang the curtain down and we had to face the wrath of Donald who almost sacked us all on the spot. It was a disgraceful exhibition and afterwards we were ashamed of ourselves, but when something like that happens one has to be superhuman not to be affected by it.

Pig in a Poke caused me more anguish than any other play I have appeared in and for the first time brought me to the edge of rebellion. The play was nonsense, everybody rushing about all over the place, with the usual misunderstandings, recriminations and reconciliations – it was, in fact, a typical English Comedy of the 1950s and hugely popular with audiences of repertory companies. I spent most of the play running on and off the stage with a pig in a pram – a *real* pig, with a frilly bonnet on its head. The idea was that the pig would be mistaken for a baby . . . The script demanded a tiny piglet but the stage manager could only come up with a much bigger specimen, not fully grown, but decidedly past the piglet stage. It sat in the pram as good as gold, seemingly smiling all over its chops, and was quite happy to be wheeled around. 'Good piggy,' we addressed it in baby language, chucking it under its massive chin. All through the play, with its shrieking and cavortings, the pig played its part excellently, and when the curtain came down and we gathered for the first call Donald, who had come backstage, said, 'Take the pig on for the call, Jean, and it will get another laugh.'

'In the pram?' I asked.

'No, no, in your arms, it will look better if you carry it on.'

So I heaved the pig out of the pram, not without trepidation, for I did not know if pigs bit or not, put one hand under its back and the other under its head, and took my place in the line-up. The pig was smiling away under its bonnet as if taking a curtain call was an everyday occurrence. The curtain went up, the audience applauded warmly, and the loud clapping together with the bright lights so startled the star of the show that it did what pigs do when they are frightened – all in my hand, all down my coat and all in my shoes . . . I was *horrified* and gazed around wildly, wondering whether to rush off or stay, and wishing that I had never left the library! The curtain went down, up again, more loud applause, a squeal from the pig and it did it all over again. We took four curtain calls and four times the pig acknowledged the acclaim. I dumped the pig in its pram in the wings, fled to the dressing room, tore off all my outer clothes and washed them and myself as quickly as possible. I smelt strongly of disinfectant when I had finished and I was subjected to a great number of coarse jokes from the male members of the company.

On Tuesday night the unthinkable happened – a repetition of the previous night's calamity, resulting in more laundry work and more accusations about smelling like a pig-sty. On Wednesday I said to Donald, 'Donald, either the pig takes the call or I take the call, but not both of us. I can't bear it *again*!'

He seemed a bit hurt. 'Why, Jean, I thought it was a good idea to hold the pig in your arms.'

'Haven't you seen what it's been doing?' I said. 'It's me or the pig. Make your choice, and I hope it can learn lines as quickly as I can,' and I stalked off.

It turned out that Donald had not seen the devastating effect of his good idea and when he learned what had been happening he agreed that the pig's shining hour should be brought to an end. A pig in a pram was fine, but a pig in my arms – no, thank you. For the rest of the week I thought I detected a touch of resentment in the way that pig looked at me and the sparkle went out of its performance.

One of the virtues of weekly Rep is that you have to be prepared for anything and to take whatever happens with complete sangfroid, from thunder sheets to spiders, from pigs to rats – and from gossiping usherettes. My brush with the latter happened during a play in which I had to deliver the contents of a long letter I'd had from my husband just before he died. 'I haven't got it with me but I know it by heart,' I had to say. I never understood why the author could not have arranged for his character to pull the letter out of a pocket and *read* it, but I suppose he thought that such a short cut would only make an actor lazy. Every time I sat facing the audience, ready to disclose the contents of the letter, I thought, 'Please, God, don't let me forget the bloody words!'

One night I had just got about halfway through when I heard whispering from behind the curtain that covered the exit door to the foyer down stage left. It got louder and turned into an argument between two usherettes about who had the key to the ladies' lavatory. 'You had it when we opened, Millie, I remember...' 'No, Florrie, I never, because you took it for Elsie to wash her hands...' 'But I'm sure you had it when Mrs Waterworth asked if she could go in...' 'No, it were open then, I'm sure...' 'I never had it, I gave it to you before we let 'em in...'

The duologue continued unabated and I was getting quite distracted, wondering where the wretched key actually was, but I ploughed on, bringing all my concentration to bear on my own dialogue. Then the voices of Millie and Florrie faded away as they retreated from the door. I breathed a sigh of relief and carried on. But my ordeal was not over. There was another door, also covered by a curtain, at the other side of the auditorium leading to a crush bar. To my horror I saw the commissionaire, in black uniform with white-topped cap, emerge from it and make his stately way down the centre gangway and across the front of the stalls in order to open the crush bar ready for the interval. My mouth was opening and words were coming out automatically as though I were a tape recorder. All I could see was the white cap; I was riveted, hypnotised by its progress. Only when the commissionaire had disappeared did I return to my character and find myself saying, 'And that was the letter that Jack wrote.' Curtain . . .

CHAPTER 11

The New House

DONALD BODLEY, our producer, had a touch of genius about him. He could coax performances out of people who did not know they were there, and in a week too. Sometimes he would drive us mad, he was so very strict; indeed, he could be a tartar at times, but there was never anything personal about his rebukes. It was not Jean Alexander who felt the lash of his tongue but an actress who was not playing as well as she could. He had the great knack of knowing just what theatre-goers wanted, what they would laugh at, cry at, be spellbound by. We did a lot of run-of-the-mill plays: we had to, working in a seaside town and having to please the summer visitors, but we did some excellent plays too: by Shakespeare, Ibsen, Wilde, Maugham and Maxwell Anderson. The actors loved doing them and a surprising number of people came to see them.

Donald would not tolerate slackness. We had to be word-perfect on the opening night and were not allowed to ad-lib unless someone had dried up completely. Everything had to be meticulously thought out in rehearsal and we would repeat a few lines of dialogue or a whole scene time and time again until he was satisfied.

Donald's appearance was unremarkable except for his eyes – very blue and piercing. They seemed to look right through the back of your head. His movements were quick and sharp, every flicker of the finger meant something important. When we were rehearsing a comedy he sat on a chair on the stage in front of us all and not a glimmer of a smile appeared on his face while we did the first run through without a script. His 'make me laugh if you dare' look was quite intimidating but it made us reach out further for comedy points and explore the text for the humour lying beneath ordinary lines.

Whatever discipline I have learned in the theatre has come from Donald Bodley. If I am a perfectionist it is because he has made me one. If I cannot bear slovenliness it is because he could not. Whatever talent I have as an actress was brought out and nurtured by him. Secondhand wasn't good enough. God knows that perfection is not achieved very often, if ever, but with Donald you were always striving for it. 'Pull your bloody selves together!' he would shout through the windows of the set if he saw any slacking or loss of concentration, any quiet giggling or deterioration of the standards he had established at rehearsal. And every night after the show we would wait on the stage until he came round to give us notes. I have known him do that even on a Saturday night after the final performance. I suppose he thought it would keep us up to scratch if we should ever do the same play again in years to come.

The permanent company at Southport was quite small, half a dozen or so, but we had people coming in for special weeks if the play needed a larger cast. Over the seven years I was there a lot of people came and went but there was a hard core, consisting of Donald and Elizabeth McKenzie, his wife, Malquitta Fermo, Stanley Lloyd, Peter Schofield, Vint Graves and myself. Noel Lloyd had left a few months after I started, to work for the Ulster Group Theatre in Belfast. Eileen Derbyshire was with us for a couple of years. Eileen is, of course, Emily Bishop in *Coronation Street*, and we were delighted to renew our friendship when I joined *The Street* several years later. We reminisced delightedly about *Uncle Harry*, in which we played two bickering sisters. One would not think, remembering the character she plays, that Eileen is one of the funniest people one could meet, and like so many of my friends, a notorious giggler. The more solemn or tragic her part the more she is exploding with laughter inside. Whenever we were feeling a bit down there was always Eileen to lift our spirits.

Whenever it was possible I would go over to Manchester on a Sunday to see my parents at the Theological College, and each time I would worry more because it was so obvious that they were unhappy. They were so pleased to see me: apart from being their only daughter I was a reminder of the Arnold Street past, when in spite of hardship they had been happy; and I would return to Southport feeling miserable and frustrated. I spoke to Ken and said, 'Look, we've got to get them out of that place – they won't last long the way things are; they're getting no fun out of life.'

Ken was sympathetic, but he was not able to help in a practical way. He was teaching all the time and had a house to keep up and a wife and two little daughters to care for. So I said to mum and dad, 'Supposing – just supposing – I could find a little house in Southport, would you come and live there, and I'd move in with you?' They knew Southport slightly, having been to some of the shows, and liked the idea of living by the sea but their response, as always, was cautious. It would have to be reasonably cheap, their savings wouldn't allow them to be reckless, then, perhaps, yes, they did like the idea . . .

Finding the right house took 18 months! Every week a friend and I would search the houses for sale columns and mark off what would be suitable in an affordable price range. Most of the places we investigated were awful and nothing like the descriptions we had been given, but one winter afternoon after tramping around for hours we came across the only house that was at all possible. It was a small semi-detached house in Sefton Street with a long garden at the back – a wilderness of old trees and overgrown bushes. Not having the keys we could only look through the windows, but what we saw made us determined to investigate further. When we eventually got inside we found it clean and newly decorated, with a warm and friendly air which seemed to say, 'Don't hesitate – buy me!' The snag was the price: £1,650. My parents' entire savings, after selling the Arnold Street house and with what they had managed to save since their marriage in 1918, were in the region of £1,200. So that's that, I thought, then immediately contradicted myself. There must be a way round the snag – I'll find it!

Mum and dad came over on Saturday. Before then I had asked the estate agent if he would hold the house until they had seen it, and he agreed. I was to ring him at his home on Saturday evening; he would get in touch with the seller and 'We'll see what happens,' he said. Mum and dad went to see the house while I was at the matinee and when I saw them after the show mum was doing her usual vacillating act – wasn't it too expensive? Perhaps we should wait a bit... I controlled my impatience admirably and pointed out that it was an ideal little house, that the opportunity was not likely to come again, and that prices were going up all the time...

'Oh, all right,' said mum at last. 'Let's go ahead and make an offer.' Dad agreed but there was still reluctance in their attitude. It would be the second big step they had taken in five years! I rang the estate agent and offered him £1,600. The seller agreed and I got a £400 mortgage which I was to repay at £3 7s 6d a month over ten years. At that stage I was earning £7 a week at the theatre, so it proved just possible. I was sorry to leave Mr and Mrs Booth but it was a relief to be really independent at last.

My parents never regretted their daring decision, I'm glad to say. Dad was about 60 when the move took place so there were a few years before he need officially retire. He did not mind what work he did as long as he was taking money home, and so he finally got a job at a small factory that made plastic dolls, where he worked until he was 67. Then there was the problem of clearing the garden of a mass of old sycamore saplings which the previous owner had not touched for 14 years. It took two years to clear it completely and we all worked very hard – with the help of Toby, our second cat.

Snooky, our beloved cat in those far-off days in Liverpool during the war, had disappeared one day from the back yard of the Arnold Street house after being with us for five years. We thought he had been stolen because, being weak in the back legs through rheumatism, he could not have got out of the yard by himself. There was a spate of catnapping in Liverpool at that time, the fur being made into gloves, and it is possible that Snooky ended up on somebody's hands. I was devastated at the time and went looking for him all over the district for days, I put notices in shop windows, but we never saw Snooky again. I missed him and his white paws and shirtfront for a long time.

Toby, who was jet black all over, was very different from Snooky. He was a real busybody, interfering in everything. He helped dad to cut down the sycamores and would sit on the end of the branch that was being sawn, watching the saw going back and forth, and then topple with it. This he could never understand. He would also jump into any hole that was being dug and get very cross when he was shooed out.

When the garden had been cleared we set a lawn with borders. Dad wanted to grow vegetables at the top end of the garden and started with lettuces. Toby was sitting watching him. Dad raked over the soil, sowed the seeds, covered them over and went to the shed for his watering-can. In the meantime Toby had rushed to the lettuce bed to see what had been buried, failed to find the hidden treasure and had scattered the soil all over the place; and when dad arrived with the watering-can Toby looked at him as if to say, 'Whatever it was you buried here I can't find it!' So that year we had lettuces coming up all over the garden.

Dear Toby was killed by a car soon after his second birthday. We did not get another cat for some months; mother had declared that there was too much heartache in loving and losing a cat, but we all felt that the family was not complete without a little furry creature to make a fuss of. So eventually Mungo arrived.

Mungo's mother was a stray tortoiseshell who used to visit people's gardens and take food from them but would never venture inside a house. We saw that she was pregnant but, soon after her babies were born she was killed by a car and nobody knew where she had hidden them. After days of searching a neighbour found them on the compost heap in his garden, blind, shivering and starving. There were four of them, three obviously in too sorry a state to survive, but the ginger one was moving . . . When mother was shown the little scrap, which was about two weeks old and not much bigger than a mouse, she said, without stopping to wonder if she was doing the sensible thing, 'I'll have it – I know Jean will want to try to rear it.'

I got back from the theatre late that evening, feeling tired, pale and wan, and went into the living-room, intending to have a hot drink and go straight to bed. I saw a shoe box in front of the fire and said listlessly, 'What's that doing there?'

'Come and see,' mum said; and when I saw the tiny thing curled up in a corner of the box I immediately fell in love!

Feeding Mungo was a problem. In the beginning he could not even lap so I dipped a finger in a milky baby cereal and rubbed it on his nose and mouth. After a few days he could lap out of a saucer but I had to hold him over the edge because the curve of the saucer was too high for him to get his nose over.

Mungo grew and grew, opened his eyes and began to take an interest in the world around him. When he was fully grown he weighed 20 pounds and could be mistaken for a marmalade dog. He ate four meals a day, apart from morning coffee, afternoon tea and Ovaltine at bedtime, and would scream the place down if there was a suggestion that he might miss a meal. We had him for 11 years and often mother would look at him, shake her head and say to him, 'I wonder why we didn't leave you on that compost heap, you greedy cat,' but in fact she adored him, as we all did, and Mungo knew it.

In 1958 I had my first holiday abroad. My friend Barbara Charles, who worked at an optician's in Southport, and I managed to save up enough money for a fortnight in Italy. In those days £28 was a vast sum and we were determined to enjoy ourselves, come what may. It took us two days to get to Laigueglia in the Bay of Alassio by land, sea and rail, and we savoured every minute of the 'abroadness'.

The fortnight itself was uneventful but I loved Italy and soaked up the sunshine like a lizard. I had heard about the expressions in fractured English that one encounters abroad and was not disappointed with those we came across. In Laigueglia there was a café in the centre of the town with tables and chairs outside on the cobbles. In the evenings the town band played and you could either dance or sit and drink at a table, or stand around at the fringe of the crowd. Outside the café there was a notice in both Italian and English. It said, 'For those sitting at the table there will be a higher charge for the first consummation of the evening.' We stood around for a while hopefully waiting for the floor show! When nothing happened we deduced that the notice meant that a cover charge would be made for the first drink to discourage anyone sitting around for the whole evening with a single drink.

There was another notice on the beach: 'Dogs and other animels (sic) must not be bathed or wetted within a hundred yards of the establishment', and on the door of the church: 'Ladies will not be admitted with bare arms or gentlemen in pyjamas or short drawers'. Again we waited, but no short-drawered Englishman who would be turned away appeared . . .

In accordance with the rules of Equity, the Actors' Trade Union, we were given one week's holiday for every consecutive six months' work. This meant that I, having been a permanent member of the Rep for so long, had two weeks' holiday a year. So there were very few opportunities to go very far afield, and the trip to Italy was the only highlight in a year of unremitting hard work. Occasionally there would be a free weekend and then Barbara and I would have a brief trip to Stratford to see a play at the Memorial Theatre and enjoy some walks in the lovely countryside.

CHAPTER 12

Moving On: York

IN THE summer of 1958 I decided to leave Southport and gave three months' notice. Donald Bodley had already left and was at York. The Rep there had been in the doldrums for some time, and if anyone could restore it to its rightful place as one of the best Reps in the country Donald could, and did. Soon there were packed houses again at practically every performance. Some people used to book the same seat for the same evening every week, and once they dropped out they never got it back again.

For some time I had been reviewing my life and thinking about my future. I had been doing a play a week for almost seven years and nearly all my parts had been long and exhausting. I was tired, drained physically and emotionally. I began to dislike the thought of Tuesdays and the rehearsals for another new play. I had very little social life and no time to make friends outside the theatre; and no opportunity for just getting up and going wherever fancy took me. My routine was getting increasingly monotonous and I hated the thought of losing my enthusiasm for the theatre.

On Monday there was the dress rehearsal and first night of the current play, the two events lasting from 10 a.m. to 10 p.m. There was rarely time for a lunch break and there were interminable waits for scenery and lighting problems to be solved. Sometimes we could not even finish the dress rehearsal before it was time for the performance; and immediately after the show Donald would give us lengthy notes on our performances.

The new play began on Tuesday at 10 a.m. We were told what parts we were playing and given scripts. We read the whole play through and blocked out the moves roughly. We broke about 2.30 p.m. and spent the rest of the afternoon learning the first act of the new play and revising the lines of the current production. There were from two to two and a half hours playing in the evening, then I would stagger home for a late supper and continue with my first act words.

On Wednesday we would rehearse the first act without scripts, and Donald was *insistent* that we did not use them. The afternoon was 'free' to learn act two. Then there was the evening performance and more learning. Thursday was 'no scripts' day for act two and learning act three in whatever time we could snatch before the performance.

We rehearsed act three without scripts on Friday morning; the rest of the day was fearsome. Acts one and two in the afternoon, and both had to be word perfect. If there was time we would snatch a quick cup of tea before the evening performance. Saturday was another hectic day. Beginning at 10 a.m. we would run through all three acts until 2 p.m., return to the theatre at 4 p.m. for the first house at 5 p.m. At 8 p.m. the curtain went up on the second house. After 11 p.m. we could actually go home . . .

Sunday was our day off! It was usually spent doing various domestic tasks, preparing costumes for the following day's dress rehearsal, more revision of lines for the whole play; then, if sanity had not entirely deserted us, we would meet friends and colleagues in the local pub for an hour or so.

And all for £8 a week . . . I weighed up the pros and cons: it was not easy. I had security of a kind, but no chance to save money. The routine had made me a quick learner and slick in getting into a new part, but what depth could one give a part in those conditions? I had found my feet as an actress, I was no longer naive and starry-eyed, I could stand up for myself (though I was still soft enough to be put upon by people like Donald!), I knew my worth, but I wanted to be worth more, to spread my wings and tackle parts that demanded more thought, exploration and polish than weekly Rep could provide opportunities for. In short, I felt rather like a perfectly acceptable duckling longing to be a swan!

When Donald left Southport the productions were taken over by Vint Graves, an elderly character actor who had been with the company for some time, a competent but uninspired producer. He was formerly in Music Hall and had been Sandy Powell's feed. Vint was very peeved when he knew I was leaving and muttered something about only going because I wanted to follow Donald to York. I tried to explain that I had had enough of weekly Rep and had given my notice to Donald before I knew he was leaving; but Vint would not accept the fact that I was innocent of any kind of duplicity, and relations were rather strained for the rest of my time at Southport.

There were at least two occasions, however, when Vint's disapproval was put to one side. He used his hands a lot as old school actors did, and claimed that in every part he played he got in a subtle V-sign that went unnoticed by the audience. In all the plays we saw him in he always did! I played a fake medium in *Crystal Clear*, a play he produced but had no part in. In one of my trances I had to say, 'The moving finger writes and having writ, moves on . . .' I illustrated the line by writing in the air with one finger and on the opening night, with Vint in the audience, I managed a slight V-sign at the end of my line, using a second finger with a delicate movement. There was a loud guffaw from one member of the audience – others looked round at him to see what was the matter.

We were doing an Agatha Christie play – thankfully we eventually reached the moment when the murderer was about to be unmasked. The police were banging on the door and the actors stood around in dead silence; horror, shock and fear flitting over their faces. In the middle of the tenseness I burped . . . Vint was standing next to me, registered the fact that there was no reaction from the audience, and muttered out of the corner of his mouth, 'H'm! That'll go better second house!' When the detective made his entrance he found a very merry band of suspects . . .

So I returned home and sat around, helping dad in the garden and mum in the house, and was depressed, not knowing what my next step ought to be. I wrote around to various companies, but received no encouraging replies, and resigned myself to a long spell of idleness. 32 years old and on the dole . . .

One day I had an unexpected visitor – Elizabeth McKenzie, Donald Bodley's wife. She was still in Southport, selling up their house before moving to York to join Donald. The reason for her call was to deliver a message from Donald, to say that if I hadn't got any work yet would I come to York for two weeks? 'No!' I wanted to shout. 'No more weekly Rep – not even for one play!' But 'Yes, please,' I said to Elizabeth, and up to York I went.

Then came a repetition of what happened at Southport. The two weeks stretched into two more, and two after that, and I stayed at York for two years, though with a couple of months break in 1960.

York provided a wonderfully stimulating change of scene but one element of my early days there was all too familiar – cats! Obsessed with the creatures I may be, but my experience at Mrs Berg's was almost enough to cure the obsession. Mrs Berg, my first landlady, was a foreign lady with a thick accent which was probably German, though I never liked to probe into her background. She lived in a big house on the outskirts of York. Among the residents were students, business people and theatricals, but the dominating presence throughout the whole house was that of cats, large, small, fat, thin, tabby, marmalade, friendly, scratchy, vigorous and lazy. It should have been an absolute paradise for me but I soon came to accept that there are limits! There must have been more than a dozen of the creatures but counting them was impossible because they would never stay in one place long enough.

The dining-room at Mrs Berg's was adjacent to her kitchen. There was one large refectory table at which we all sat for meals and a smaller table at the other end of the room which held the largest teapot I have ever seen. It must have held at least a gallon. Over the teapot there was a knitted tea-cosy as big as a pullover. The drill was to help yourself to a cup of tea then sit at the big table with the others. On my first morning I duly went to pour out my tea but before lifting the cosy I realised that a large black and tan cat was sitting on top of it, forepaws folded over the spout and the rest of it draped over the pot. It made no attempt to move as I approached and even gave me a challenging glare. I lifted it off the cosy, placed it on the table while I poured the tea, then put back the cosy, carefully lifted up the cat and replaced it on top of the pot. It gave a little purr of approval as I moved away, complimenting me for being quick on the uptake.

There were cats all over the house, sitting like statues in the strangest places and following one's every movement with their bright eyes. Sometimes I failed to notice one sitting on a window ledge or partly concealed behind a curtain. The staircase banister had a square newel-post and often a cat would be perched on top of it as I went upstairs. At first I thought it was a pottery ornament, then it jumped down and bounded on ahead. There was something quite sinister about the way they would slink round the house, parking themselves when and where they fancied. It was as if they controlled the house and we humans were only there on sufferance. They seemed to be especially conscious of my presence and seemed to go out of their way to gather round me. It may have been that I communicated with them in some way unknown to me. I remembered what a local theatre critic had written about my performance in *Aladdin*:

'Jean Alexander gives convincing proof that Pythagoras was right after all, and there is something in the theory of the transmigration of souls . . . for, if she was not a cat in a previous existence, it is difficult to see how she has gained such knowledge of feline habits. Her performance as Sammy the Cat is the most feline thing since Felix stopped walking'.

Rather oddly expressed, perhaps, but an acceptable tribute to my acting or an inspired perception of my cat-like qualities.

I only stayed at Mrs Berg's for a few weeks. I found that I did not care for such a communal existence; I would prefer more privacy. I could not afford to rent a flat on my own so I joined forces with Jane Dodworth, the scenic artist, and Beryl Bunn, her assistant, and we searched the local paper for addresses of furnished flats to let. Soon we were successful in finding one in Bootham Grange, quite near to the theatre. It was at the top of a large house and was owned by two elderly sisters who lived there for nine months of the year and went abroad for the three winter months. They could not stand the harsh English winters and probably could not stand each other after nine months together, for one went to the West Indies, and the other to Majorca! They let the flat fully furnished for the three months they were away, and after we had visited them and been vetted over afternoon tea they agreed that we could take the flat.

It was a very grand place, full of antique furniture. There was a

Sheraton dining suite, an Elizabethan writing desk, a carved Stuart chest and a dresser on which there was a whole Wedgwood dinner service. We looked and admired – and we were *terrified*. 'Beryl,' I said firmly, for she was notoriously accident-prone, 'we don't touch anything on that dresser – right?'

Beryl nodded. 'Woolworth's, here we come,' she murmured.

There was another aspect of the flat that proved to be more disturbing than the risk of breakages. It was haunted . . .

I got home from the theatre one Saturday night, leaving Jane and Beryl at the weekly ritual of taking down the set, and I knew they would be late back. I had a snack then washed my hair. I was sitting in the kitchen, my head wrapped in a towel, when I heard the front door of the flat open and footsteps coming along the hall. They stopped suddenly just outside the kitchen. I looked at my watch – it was just after midnight. Very early for Jane and Beryl, I thought. I called out, 'Jane, is that you?' There was no reply. I looked in the bathroom. It was empty. By this time I was puzzled and a bit worried. I crept into the drawing-room and from the fireplace picked up a big brass poker with a lethal-looking knob at the end and continued my tour. I threw open the door of a boxroom. 'Come out, whoever you are,' I called out loudly, sounding braver than I felt. Then, poker at the ready, I went through all the rooms again, looking under beds and in wardrobes and behind curtains. All I aroused was dust. I went to bed feeling rather foolish and I said nothing to the other girls when I saw them the following morning.

A couple of weeks later Beryl was having a night off. 'I'm going to indulge myself,' she said. 'I'll light a fire and listen to my records.'

But as I was going to my dressing-room in the second interval that night I spotted Beryl in the wings talking to Jane. 'Whatever happened to the lazy evening?' I said.

Beryl gave a shudder. 'I'm not staying in that flat on my own.'

'Why?' I asked, and it dawned on me what she was going to say.

'The front door opened and somebody came in. I'm sure of it. There were footsteps that stopped. I knew it wasn't either of you, so I fled!' Beryl looked quite shaken. Then Jane said, 'You know, it's odd. I've heard the same kind of noise when I've been alone in the flat.'

'Yes, it is odd because I've heard it too,' I said. The three of us gazed at each other, then shrugged our shoulders and dismissed the matter for the time being.

My mother came to stay with us a week or so later. On her first night she came to see the show, the next night we had to leave her in the flat. I was not totally surprised when she turned up at the theatre later in the evening. 'It's a funny flat, that,' she said. 'Somebody came in and went out again without a word. It gave me quite a turn and I decided I wasn't going to stay there on my own.'

So that made four of us who had had the same experience, but always separately. Disturbing though it all was, none of us felt menaced in any way. It was almost as if someone needed reassurance and comfort, someone needed company. At the end of the three months we had heard the footsteps several times, but always when one of us was alone, and we became used to them. We wished that something or someone would materialise, but nothing ever did.

When the old ladies returned and we handed over our keys I said, quite bluntly, 'Do you ever hear anything strange in this flat?'

One of them gave a chuckle. 'Goodness me, have you heard our ghost?'

'All three of us, and my mother,' I said.

'I suppose I should have warned you, but I completely forgot,' the old lady said. 'As you have discovered it never actually does anything, it is quite harmless.'

'But who is it?' I asked.

The old lady shook her head. 'We don't know, and there are no means of finding out. He – or she – has been here as long as we have. We did hear a story about the daughter of a former owner of the house, before it was turned into flats, who was confined to this top floor to keep her away from her lover. Eventually she died of a broken heart. But it was only a story told by an old man who lived in the basement and who was not always sober. I don't suppose for a moment anything like that really happened.'

That is my only experience of ghosts. Now I don't know what to believe. Was there a poor girl looking for her lover? If so, I hope she found him . . .

The Theatre Royal at York was a beautiful building, all wedding-cake white, gold and crimson. It was always very well kept and the velvet seats looked as pristine as they were comfortable. The seating capacity was quite large; it had a grand circle and an upper circle; the sight lines and acoustics were excellent. One can sense when playing whether or not the voice is reaching to the most distant points and this aspect made it an enjoyable theatre to play in. It had a big stage and more than adequate wing-space so we were never cramped, which was a luxury in itself.

I love York dearly and think of it as my second home. There is so much to do and see: the glories of the Minster, superb museums, fine shops, the constant excavations, the city walks and snickelways and the nearness of the Yorkshire moors and dales. Then there are Rievaulx Abbey, Fountains Abbey, Helmsley – all delightful places to visit. Today I frequently go back to York to see the friends I made during my theatre days there, particularly Joyce Kay.

Joyce was a primary school teacher, retired now for many years, who was interested in all the arts, but had a special love for the theatre. She had always been a regular patron of the Theatre Royal and in the course of time had become friendly with both actors and staff. She loved to help out backstage, assisting at quick changes, running repairs, finding props – 'Ask Joyce' was heard around the theatre as often as 'What's the time?' She had been invaluable in this way years before I came on the scene but I soon got to know her, particularly when we did the first York Revue towards the end of my first year there.

As a change from a weekly play Donald arranged a programme of songs, sketches and monologues which he culled from famous London revues such as *Sweeter and Lower* and *The Lyric Revue*, written by Alan Melville, Flanders and Swan and Arthur Macrae. This we did for a fortnight and both we and the audiences enjoyed it tremendously. We appreciated the chance to let our hair down and some of us showed a previously unsuspected talent for singing and dancing. My dancing turned out to be better than my singing . . .

The revue was two weeks of very hard work and we could not have got through it without Joyce's help. There were a great many quick changes and she had a rail of clothes in the wings. She knew exactly what costume to have ready for the next item and she would help us to undress with the speed of light and put on the next costume with equal efficiency. I'm sure she worked harder backstage than we did onstage.

Joyce and I became firm friends and she often stayed with us in Southport. When my mother decided that she was too old to go on long trips to distant places, and knowing that I preferred not to travel alone, she said, 'Take Joyce with you, you'll have a marvellous time together.' Joyce agreed enthusiastically and since then we have been on many holidays together. We have explored the Mediterranean thoroughly, visiting Corfu, Sicily, the Greek Islands, Malta, Gibraltar, Cyprus, Athens, Naples, Sorrento, Pompeii and Palermo; and further afield we have been to Jerusalem, Istanbul, Cairo, Tangiers, and the West Indies. My longing for the colourful and the romantic will never be satisfied, I fear, and as long as there is a ship ready to take me to exotic places I will be on it.

One of the items in the York Revue was a Victorian Music Hall number. I did the Marie Lloyd song *Don't dilly dally on the way*, wearing an elaborately feathered hat, an over-decorated Victorian dress with the obligatory feather boa, and I carried a birdcage containing a stuffed canary on a perch. I began the song with all the panache I could muster and all went well until I began the last chorus:

'My old man said, 'Follow the van
Don't dilly dally on the way –'
Off went the cart with the home packed in it,
I walked be'ind with me old cock linnet . . .'

At this point the seed cage fell from the cage on to the floor. I pretended not to notice, and went on:

'But I dillied and dallied, dallied and dillied,
Lost the van and don't know where to roam . . .'

Right on cue, out fell the water pot and hit the stage with a ping.

'You can't trust the specials like the old time coppers . . .'

The bird fell off its perch.

'When you can't find your way 'ome.'

On the last word the top loop by which I was holding the cage came loose and the whole cage collapsed in front of me. As each incident occurred the audience gave a chuckle, then a longer laugh, and finally they burst into applause. They thought it was deliberate, but of course it was not, and I was quite shaken as the cage disintegrated bit by bit. The reception was gratifying but I could never make it happen again, with every incident bang on cue, so I decided not to try. It was a lovely accident, but unrepeatable.

What happened during the *Bellringers* number did not have quite such a happy ending. There were four of us in the item, each with a bellrope ringing different toned bells. Jimmy Beck, George Woolley, Josie Kidd and I were the ringers; the pay-off to the number left us all in the air clinging to our ropes until a black-out and curtain brought the scene to an end. This was to be achieved by putting a foot into a special loop at the bottom of the rope just before we were to be flown, that is pulled, about ten feet up into the air. There we would hang until the curtains swung across after the blackout. Then we would be lowered to the stage while a short front cloth act took place. The sequence of events was clear to us all and the fact that no flyman had been available at rehearsal did not worry us unduly.

When the time came we performed the sketch, found the prepared foot loop, delivered the last line and, sure enough, up we all went. I heard a thump – Jimmy was safely down; another thump, George had landed, another, Josie was down, but I, instead of following them, felt myself going, not down, but up! My flyman must have been too long in the pub. 'Down,' I hissed at him, 'let me down, you fool . . .' 'Oh, sorry,' I heard him call, and I went up even higher. It was still pitch dark and I had no idea how high I had been pulled except that it felt like *miles*.

'Down, please will you let me down!' I called, beginning to get panicky. I knew that the front cloth number was quite short and that I had a clothes change before the next sketch. I wondered if I could let myself down hand over hand, like we had to do at school in gym: at which point I found myself clutching a handful of curtain and realised that the rope had swung as the curtain had swished across after the blackout and that I was hanging in front of the black velvet tabs instead of behind them! I was on the audience side . . . A quick decision – I slid down the rope, burning my hands in the process, until I got to the loop at the foot and found that my feet were still not on the stage. What to do now? I thought I would have to trust to luck and just drop to the ground, however far beneath me it was. So I gritted my teeth and let go – and fell about six inches. To me it seemed like six feet, and the jarring to my spine made me use the first epithet that came into my mind. 'SHIT!' I shouted at the top of my voice and fought my way back through the curtains just as the lights came up. Not very ladylike, but very comforting. The audience heard, of course, but I hoped that they would not know the identity of the culprit. The whole incident was very brief but to me it seemed endless. Afterwards I wondered if I should have stayed hanging there until the lights came up. I would have looked so ludicrous suspended in mid-air, it would surely have brought the house down.

As for the flyman who had aroused such murderous thoughts in me, one of his mates said later, 'You can't blame him really, he'd never done the job before!'

'*Now* you tell me,' I said.

Eugene O'Neill's *Anna Christie* is a play we did at York that I remember with affection. I played the old bargewoman called Marty (Marie Dressler played her in the Greta Garbo film) who only appeared for fifteen minutes at the beginning of the play. It was a challenging part – small, slim Jean Alexander pretending to be a large old lady. But I padded myself till I was quite enormous, and wore an ancient skirt, a man's jacket and cap, and boots that Jeffery Dench lent me. And my make-up was a triumph, though I say it myself, and it took hours to put on.

My only appearance was in the bar room scene and during the fifteen minutes I was on stage I had to smoke a pipe, spit in the spittoon (accurately), hold a long conversation with Jeffery Dench, who was playing Chris Christopherson, and drink three pints of stout – *real* stout. You can't fake stout – it is impossible to get a head on it nor can you get it black enough. Besides, drinking three pints of some awful concoction would have had dire results – not that the stout didn't. I was given a glass tankard to drink from, not a pewter one, so I could not just pretend to drink. Down it all had to go, three pints in fifteen minutes – six pints on Saturdays.

There were so many scene changes in the play that a number of platforms on wheels – called trucks – were used, and of course if you were on a truck for a scene you were above the actual stage level. Every night I gallantly drank my stout, finished my speech, got to the door of the set, delivered my parting shot, shut the door behind me, forgot the distance from truck to stage and fell flat on my face. Every night I would crawl to my dressing-room drunk as a lord. It was lucky that I had no other scene in the play. The drink seemed to have a cumulative effect and by Wednesday I was in a semi-coma. Gallons of black coffee helped to sober me up before Friday, which was the evening my parents were coming from Southport to see the show.

They came to the stage door where I was waiting to give them their tickets, in full costume and make-up. Dad looked at me as I held them out, nodded vaguely and let mum take them. 'Goodness, look at you,' she said.

'I'll see you after the show,' I said. 'Hope you enjoy it.'

When I had gone dad asked, 'Who was that?'

'Your one and only daughter,' mum replied.

'Good God,' he said, and his mouth fell open. 'Our Jean . . .'

I had been at York for nearly two years before I decided to leave. It was the Southport situation all over again. I was tired. I had enjoyed the experience tremendously, done good plays and made some marvellous friends. York was a very pleasant place in which to live and work. So why wasn't I really happy? The answer was that old devil ambition was stirring in me again. I had certainly spread my wings with this company, but I felt they were not fully extended. Somewhere in the wide world there must be greater opportunities, greater heights; and that somewhere was, of course, London.

I was going to miss some lovely people. James Beck was one. We had become firm friends and later I stayed with him and his wife in London. Jimmy was brilliant as the spiv in *Dad's Army* and his sudden death was a tragedy for his family and friends, and the theatre lost a fine actor. Trevor Bannister was also at York. He later starred in *Are You Being Served?* Jeffery Dench, who joined the Royal Shakespeare Company, Josie Kidd, Beth Harris, Brian Mosley (with whom I had a joyful reunion when we met again in *Coronation Street*, he as Alf Roberts), all helped to make my life enjoyable, and I must mention June Barry particularly. She is now one of my very best friends.

I left York in January, 1960, returned home and sat there for two months. I had intended to go to London but my savings, such as they were, were gradually dwindling away and it would have been foolhardy to descend on the capital with no job, no prospects, no connections and with about sixpence in my purse.

In April, in response to a letter, an offer came from the Liverpool Playhouse, a six weeks' engagement to play in *Quality Street*, J.M. Barrie's play which was being produced to mark the centenary of his birth. The offer came from Willard Stoker, the director I had admired from afar for many years, and to work with him, even for a short time, would be a high point of my career. I remembered well the many evenings I had spent in that theatre, longing to be an actress, and now I had been specially chosen to tread those very boards!

I played Miss Mary Willougby. Caroline Blakiston was Phoebe Throssel, and Rita Tushingham and Benjamin Whitrow were also in the cast. The luxury of rehearsing for three weeks was a new and welcome experience, and the six weeks passed all too quickly. The production was polished and elegant and not a thing went wrong!

When the Liverpool engagement came to an end I went to Harrogate for a special week to do two little Grand Guignol plays. Halfway through the week Donald Bodley telephoned from York. Somebody had let him down and would I go back to play in *Roar Like a Dove* which was to open the following Monday? I had to learn the part on Saturday and Sunday, get to York and rehearse on Monday right up to opening time. Somehow I did it. It is amazing how stimulating excessive pressure can be. Wily Donald then asked me to stay on and I weakly agreed. But it was only for eight months and in 1961 I gave up the treadmill of weekly Rep for *good*.

John Barrie and York and I had a brief entanglement. We had met at Oldham, then again at York when my first week was his last, but he occasionally came back during the next two years to see Jimmy, Jeffery, and Trevor. He would watch the show and join us afterwards for a drink. So I got to know him, though not very well. 'Jean,' he said to me one night, 'I've seen your work and it's good. You ought to get away from this slavery and get on telly . . .'

'How I've tried,' I said. 'I've written letters to everyone I can think of, but I've only worked in the provinces and nobody wants to know. I think I'm stuck with Rep for ever.'

'Now listen to me,' he said. 'Get yourself down to London. I'll put you in touch with my agent – she knows I wouldn't recommend anyone I didn't think was worth it. I'm sure she'll take you on. Then the rest will be up to you.' He talked so seriously and encouragingly that, willy-nilly, my mind was made up for me.

Soon afterwards I caught a bad dose of flu and had to go home. Donald agreed reluctantly that I could not really act with a temperature, aching limbs and no voice. Jimmy Beck left York while I was away, and when I had recovered I put myself, with all my possessions and with £70 in my purse, on a train to London on a cold January morning in 1961. True to his word John Barrie introduced me to Joan Reddin, his agent. She agreed, perhaps a little hesitantly because she had never seen my work, to put me on her books and said she would do her best for me. I have been with Joan ever since, nearly thirty years. We have grown old together! She was red-haired, like me, and Irish with it. We liked each other on sight and we still do . . .

There are three people who have been instrumental in helping me to achieve whatever success I have had in my career; their actions have resulted in my being able to haul myself from one step up the ladder to another. Perhaps I would have been lucky in other ways and still got to the top. I don't know. I shall always be grateful to three good friends: Rene Edwards for introducing me to the professional theatre by way of the Adelphi Guild Theatre; Noel Lloyd for recommending me to Donald Bodley and giving me the opportunity to perfect my craft in weekly Rep; and John Barrie, whose generous espousal of my cause opened up the world of TV to a stranger from the provinces.

CHAPTER 13

Provincial Lady in London

MY ARRIVAL in London caused no great stir, no shooting stars or outbreak of Northern Lights. The city could not have cared less whether I was there or not. I suppose there was a touch of arrogance in my reaction: 'I'll make you care – one day . . .'

Trevor Bannister and his wife put me up for the first few nights, but they could only provide a camp bed in the sitting-room of their small flat and I knew I must go searching for a place of my own very soon. But the luck that has pursued me throughout my life caught up with me again, and more fairy god-parents appeared – Jimmy and Kay Beck. By chance they came to visit the Bannisters, saw my plight and with one voice said, 'We've got a spare room, come and stay with us.' I needed no second invitation and stayed with them for about 18 months.

The Labour Exchange I attended for my twice weekly signing was in Berwick Market. I walked there from wherever I was living, first from Chelsea, then when Jimmy and Kay moved, from Queen's Gate Terrace near the Albert Memorial. My dole money was £4 17s 6d a week, and as the bus or tube fare would have been sixpence each way I chose to walk. After signing on I would spend the rest of the day walking all over London. With the help of the *A to Z* I took a different area on each occasion and explored the town thoroughly. Sometimes I would find myself a long way from home at the end of an exhausting tramp but I always resisted the temptation to catch a bus. Occasionally I would meet a theatrical chum at the Labour Exchange, the Berwick Market branch was famous for the number of resting actors on its books, and if it was Friday, when we got our money, we would treat ourselves to coffee and a bun at Lyons' Corner House. For two years my main meal of the day was macaroni cheese, or something similar . . .

During my first three months in London I had a lot of interviews with the casting directors of various TV companies, all arranged by Joan Reddin. I wanted so much to be worthy of her trust and that, of course, of John Barrie, and I was delighted when I got my first part in a TV series called *Deadline Midnight*, in April. It was a small part but it lasted for three weeks and I got £54 for it – the most money I had ever earned in my life: it worked out at £18 a week. I played a mother, my daughter being Anna Cropper who, I later discovered, was William Roache's wife. Glyn Houston was also in the cast. I remember little about the experience except that I spent the whole time with my eyes and ears open, absorbing all I could gather about this (to me) new and exciting medium.

Two months later I got another small part in a TV play called *A Different Drum*. It was about a boys' school and, not surprisingly, I played the part of the mother of one of the boys. We rehearsed in a Boys' Club in Fulham which had a snooker table in the recreation room. Snooker has always been one of my favourite pastimes so I enjoyed any free time we had improving my performance. Douglas Wilmer was one of the teachers; another was Eric Portman.

Eric Portman – one of my heroes in the theatre! I shall never forget *His Excellency* or *The Browning Version*. I was fully resigned to worshipping him from afar, but it all worked out very differently. Most of the cast used to have a proper lunch at a nearby hotel, but I could only afford a sandwich so I found a nice unpretentious little pub and would sit down at an outside table with my sandwich and half pint of bitter. Who should come along one day but Eric Portman, and what is more, he stopped! 'How nice to see you,' he said. 'Why don't you go to the hotel for lunch with the others?'

There was no point in pretending. 'I can't afford it,' I said with a brave smile.

His response was, 'What are you drinking?' and soon he was sitting beside me and we were chatting as though we had known each other for years. I could not understand why he should pick on a humble person like me to be friendly with, but I was content to enjoy the experience. I must have had some quality that struck a chord in him, perhaps because we were both Northerners. Every morning after rehearsal he would meet me at the door and say, 'If you're going along to the pub I'll see you there.' He was a very charming man.

The last rehearsal before the recording took place at Rediffusion's headquarters in the old Air Ministry building in Aldwych. I was going down in the lift at the end of the session, all ready to walk home, when Eric Portman got in. 'Hello, Jean, are you in a hurry? My car won't be here for a while so come and have a drink. I know a nice little place round the corner.' I said my thanks and accompanied him to 'the nice little place'. It was only the Waldorf Hotel – and there was I in summer cotton dress and sandals. 'Eric, I can't go in there,' I said in alarm, 'not dressed like this!'

'Nothing wrong with your dress,' he said, 'and if they don't like it they can lump it,' and he marched me into the cocktail lounge. And with Eric it did not seem to matter that I was not in a little slinky black number. It was 20 years before I went into the Waldorf Hotel again.

My next part was also a small one, in a comedy series called *Winning Widows*, starring Peggy Mount. It was only for a week, but I had another experience of the kindness of a star towards a small part player. Peggy Mount somehow got to know that I lived in Queen's Gate Terrace and that I always walked to and from Kentish Town, where we were rehearsing. She had to go in that direction herself so she arranged to pick me up opposite the Science Museum every morning to give me a lift in her car. She need not have done so, but she was a very good-natured lady and I grew very fond of her.

September saw me getting my next job – in *Jacks and Knaves*, with John Barrie, the first time we had actually worked together. There were four episodes altogether, each a different story about the Police Force. The series eventually developed into *Z Cars*. My part lasted for three weeks and brought me £69: my weekly salary (when there was one at all) had now risen to £23. If only I could have earned that amount every week!

In October I appeared in my first film, as opposed to TV filming – a walk-on part in *The Castaways*, being shot at Pinewood. It lasted only two days. Getting to Pinewood by 7.30 a.m. meant rising at some unearthly hour, trudging to the station, suffering a dreary journey and returning at night by the same route. As I was in the throes of a heavy cold I decided to be very daring and hire a car to take me there. I knew that I would be getting £40 for the two days and the car would only cost £8 a day so I would not lose out in the end. It felt good, arriving at Pinewood Studios in a gorgeous limousine driven by a uniformed chauffeur – I almost forgot that I did not have a single word to say. Maurice Chevalier was in the film. I was walking down a long corridor back to the set after lunch, dressed in a heavy Victorian costume. In front of me Chevalier was just about to open a door. He heard me approaching, opened the door, smiled and bowed in that lovely French way, his blue eyes sparkling, and waved me through before him. At that moment I would not have changed places with the Queen of England!

It was not long before a really lucky break came, a part in a BBC series called *Television Club* which went out in the afternoon with a repeat the following morning. The first series lasted from January to May, 1962, and I got £25 per episode; there was a second series the following year. For the first time since leaving York I began to feel secure, and was able to have my shoes repaired! I could pay my rent without causing too great a hole in my money, and occasionally a pound would go into my Post Office bank. The future was certainly not rosy yet but it was tinged with a delicate pink that held out promise for the future.

The stories were centred round a family of mother, father and two children (I played the mother and Bernard Kay the father) and their adventures in various aspects of daily life; it had a decidedly educational aim. Once we 'bought' a new dining-room suite in order to explain how hire purchase works; on another occasion we were shown how a sewage farm operates. It was all very worthy and rather dull. My first location filming took place on a cold February day with intermittent snow showers. We, the family, were on an Easter trip on the Thames in a pleasure boat. We were in the middle of the river near Westminster Pier. Bernard Kay and I were sitting on one of the seats chatting away and the cameraman was perched on the ship's rail with a hand-held camera, his assistant holding on to his legs. Just as he was about to film a great flurry of snow came along and spoilt the shot.

The cameraman swore and the rest of us relaxed. The snow stopped and we got set up again. More snow . . . This happened several times. When the snow finally decided to call it a day and the words, 'right, roll it,' were said, I opened my mouth to say the first line. Something fell in front of my eyes. There was a seagull's squawk and a great splodge on my lap. I looked up at the bird, shook my fist at it and called out, 'You dirty bugger, you might have waited!' The cameraman started to laugh and would have gone head first into the Thames if his assistant had not been holding his legs.

Another film location was Blackpool, where the family was to spend a week's holiday. First we were seen arriving at Blackpool Station alighting from the train. One already standing in the station was used for getting out of the carriage, but then we had to be filmed going down the platform, mingling with the other passengers and handing our tickets to the collector at the barrier. An excursion train was just due in, so the cameras were set up at the end of the platform. It duly arrived, passengers began to pour out and we were given our cue to join the crowd on its trek to the barrier, when a woman with a little boy spotted the camera. She dragged the boy up to it and said challengingly, 'Come on, George, we'll get the man to take your photo.' 'Cut', said the director. By this time the platform was practically empty and we had to wait two hours for another excursion train to arrive – this time thankfully without George and his mother.

Another scene was shot at the top of Blackpool Tower. There is not a lot of room on the top gallery which is enclosed by iron railings and which to me didn't look too safe. Bernard and I had to lean against the railings looking out over the town below us. The tower was swaying in the wind and my vertigo, which is like having toothache all the way from my head to my feet, left me dizzy and sick. 'Bernard,' I said as the familiar ache began to gnaw at me, 'for goodness sake hang on to my coat or I shall jump off!' Height is like a magnet, it pulls me down. My knuckles were white and my teeth were chattering. Bernard gripped my coat and I clung to the railings, but not too hard because I was convinced they might break and I would be propelled downwards to the ground. The filming took an hour and when I had reached ground level I hurried away to be sick.

Several times since then, during my *Coronation Street* days, I have had to work from a height, not as far up as the Blackpool Tower, but when I hung out of a first floor window and shouted to someone in the street below it used to bring on an attack of vertigo and if a prop man had not held on to my legs I would have jumped out, the compulsion was so strong.

In one episode of *Television Club* the family went for a day trip to Le Havre – this was to show the young viewer how to use a passport, deal with the Customs and how to appreciate the differences between the English way of life and the French. We were about to film a scene about crossing the road, obedience to the traffic policeman and penalties for jay-walking. The camera was set up on the corner of a road and a couple of policemen stood out of camera range to make sure we were doing all we should. Just as we were about to obey the director's call to action a police inspector approached with slow and dignified tread like one of the Bold Gendarmes. With lots of gold braid all over him and highly polished boots he looked both elegant and impressive. Although everything was going well he wanted to impress the English with French efficiency so he disrupted the proceedings in order to talk to the director and cameraman, waved his hands, nodded his head sagely and gave the impression of a French general reviewing his troops.

At the height of his pompous discourse an elderly Frenchman dragging an Alsatian dog on a chain stopped by the camera, looked it up and down and demanded to know what was going on and why couldn't he use that spot, his usual spot, to cross the road. The inspector assumed an even more officious air and waved the citizen on his way. An argument developed which steadily grew more heated. The old man was evidently asserting his rights as a rate-payer and a patriotic Frenchman to stand where he chose to stand, cross where he chose to cross, and no foreign rubbish was going to stop him. The inspector did not agree. The foreigners had been given permission to set their cameras up in the street, they were guests of La France, and that was that. The man would not move and the inspector began to behave like a bottle of champagne about to blow its top. The dog, meanwhile, was getting more and more bored, yawning, whining and pulling at its lead. As a final protest it cocked its leg against the inspector's boots and peed all over them.

The inspector went purple, the elderly man took one look at what his dog had done, hauled on its chain and was away up the road as fast as his bent old legs would take him; and the inspector whipped out his notebook and went after the criminal and its accessory. He had lost face in front of illustrious visitors and someone would have to pay for it dearly. It was like a scene from a Jacques Tati film and we all nipped round the corner and into a shop doorway to hide our helpless laughter.

By the time the second series of *Television Club* went out, from January to May, 1963, I was actually beginning to make a small name for myself and younger people recognised me in the street because the series was shown in a great number of schools. I did not receive the same attention as in later years when Hilda Ogden was such a familiar face, but such small recognition was gratifying to someone who had been out of work on and off for a couple of years and was likely to be so again when the current job ended. I did not get big-headed then, nor have I ever.

I had a week off from the series and went to York to stay with Joyce. I was looking round the Minster when I was spotted by one of a group of about forty schoolgirls, real St Trinian's types, being shown around by a teacher. She nudged her chums, they all looked in my direction, then swooped down on me like a lot of crows. I moved away quickly. The teacher was clearly furious and I grew more and more embarrassed as the girls followed me up and down the aisles, behind pillars and screens and in and out of lady chapels. The clattering of feet and excited chattering made other visitors stare and frown and I began to feel as though I were trying to escape from the avenging Furies. At last I stopped suddenly and was nearly knocked over by a gaggle of girls, all waving scraps of paper, coming to a halt in front of me. 'Girls!' I said in what I hoped was a schoolmistressy way. 'We can't have this sort of behaviour in the Cathedral. If you want my autograph I'll meet you outside when your tour is over.'

'OK,' they chorused and turned back to their grim-faced teacher.

'I'm sorry,' I began, but she ignored me.

'This way, girls, in an orderly line, if you please. *Hush*, Brenda!'

I waited for the class outside the Minster as promised and duly obliged them with my autograph. 'It wasn't my fault,' I explained to the teacher. 'I did try to keep away from them but they've seen me on TV –'

She sniffed but grudgingly admitted that the girls were to blame for the excitement. They all moved away and I was left pondering on the penalties of popularity. Signing my name 40 times in a few minutes was a new experience. I did not expect that it would ever happen again . . .

After the first series of *Television Club* I did an episode of *Z Cars*; in fact, I did four *Z Cars* altogether during my London years – all different parts and now all blurred in my memory; though I know I enjoyed meeting Jeremy Kemp, Jimmy Ellis, Stratford Johns, Brian Blessed and Frank Windsor. At that time *Z Cars* went out live, and that was a hair-raising experience. In live television anything that goes wrong stays wrong, and all the filmed bits had to be slotted in between the studio sequences while the scene was in progress. It kept us all on our toes for the whole episode.

I was still staying with Jimmy and Kay at Queen's Gate Terrace, and although they continued to be very friendly and welcoming and did not for a moment hint that my presence was in any way an intrusion, I did begin to feel that perhaps I had enjoyed their hospitality long enough, even though I was paying rent and had my own small bedroom to retire to if they had visitors or wanted to be alone.

The opportunity to give them their freedom came when two friends from my York days, Michael Gover and Charles Herdman, offered me accommodation in the large furnished flat in Cromwell Road they had just taken. The rent of the flat was 18 guineas a week, so we each had to find six guineas. Michael and Charles were working and could afford it. I was only working spasmodically so it would be harder for me but I determined to find my share somehow. Sunday lunch was included, so that was a help; and one evening during the week I would cook dinner for the three of us. I was invited to watch their TV whenever I wanted, and we all went out for drinks occasionally. It was ideal for me and I don't think I could have stayed in London as long as I did had it not been for those two. I think they enjoyed having me there; we seemed to share the same sense of humour, a bit caustic and a bit crude. Long afterwards, when I worked for Granada, we would visit each other. Michael died last year but Charles still comes up to Southport to see me.

Now I have to record something that very few people know about or, if they once did, have forgotten. I appeared in *Coronation Street* long before I became Hilda Ogden! Only once and only for a week. It was in October, 1962. Harry Hewitt and his wife Concepta were celebrating their wedding anniversary when their baby Christopher was kidnapped from outside Gamma Garments, having been left there in his pram by Lucille Hewitt. Elsie Tanner tracked down the baby and recovered him from his kidnapper, Joan Akers, played by Anna Cropper. My part was that of the landlady of the house in which Joan Akers lived. It was not a part that caused any stir, and I returned to London without any hope that the series would ever see me again. Still, I had acted with some of the stars of *The Street*, and that was something.

Other engagements in those lean years included a small part in a TV play called *Heart to Heart*. Kenneth More, Angela Baddeley, Wendy Craig and Ralph Richardson were in it, and it was good to rub shoulders with such famous people. After the second series of *Television Club* I paid a second visit to Granada in Manchester. They were doing four adaptations of de Maupassant short stories. The episode I was in had the same plot as *The Dear Departed*, the play I had produced under Miss Potter's guidance all those years ago. So the wheel spins . . . Then came another play for the BBC called *The Way With Reggie*. It is only worth mentioning because I played Michael Caine's mother. He was not so well known then, but I can boast that he has been my most famous 'son'.

In 1963 June Barry got married to David Whittaker, writer and actor. I had never lost touch with her since our York days and we often met in London. In 1961 she had written to tell me that she was joining the cast of *Coronation Street*, the new series that was expected to last 13 weeks, playing Annie Walker's daughter Joan; and I was very pleased for her. She was in the first six episodes then got married (in the story) and went to live in Derby. So that was the end of her *Street* days. When the character re-appeared briefly some years afterwards it was played by another actress.

I was invited to the wedding and to the reception at the De Vere Hotel in Kensington, just opposite Kensington Gardens. I spent a week wondering what to wear. Still barely able to save on my infrequent fees I was living in my old clothes, good enough for rehearsals and pottering about in, but not really suitable for a rather grand wedding. I raked the town for something reasonably smart and not too expensive, and finally saw a little dress shop in Oxford Street, where I found a dress and full length coat in a summer material. It had a white background covered with brown and cream leaves, rather fashionable at the time, but the snag was, it was 12 guineas, rather more than I wanted to pay. I'd never spent that much on a dress before and for a time I hesitated. Then 'Hell,' I said, 'It's elegant – hang the expense, I'll get it!'

Looking, I hoped, as though I walked in and out of the De Vere Hotel every day of my life I strolled up the steps to the main door. Standing on the doorstep was a woman waiting for her husband, who was parking their car, and she was wearing a frock and coat exactly like mine! For a moment there was a flash of antagonism between us, then we both laughed. I said, 'Snap!' and she said, 'Never mind,' and we both entered the hotel and took our places in the reception line, making sure that we were separated by a number of people.

But wherever I went in that reception room, my doppelgänger was beside me, behind me, in front of me, back to back: it seemed that those dresses had built-in magnets. When it became obvious that we were doomed to keep bumping into each other we decided to submit.

'Where did you get yours?' she asked.

'In Oxford Street,' I replied. 'It cost me 12 guineas.'

She gave a little gasp. 'Mine was from Barker's, and it cost me 14!'

The next time I wore that dress was in September, 1969 in *Coronation Street*, at Albert Tatlock's wedding that never was. Many of the things that I wore in the programme were either my own or my mother's; things that were a bit big looked better on Hilda, making her thinner but more sloppy. The famous tent coat was the one the seagull used for target practice during the filming of the *Television Club* episode on the Thames, and the old red mac was one I bought in Southport in 1956 and wore in many plays at the Scala Theatre. It was fearfully smart in those days, but it suited Hilda down to the ground ten years later. I wore it in my very first entrance in *The Street* and it stayed in the

In my role as mascot for a Welsh Rugby team

Hilda with *Coronation Street's* Bobby

Being presented to the Queen, Palace Theatre, Manchester (1977)

With Sir John Betjeman

A studio portrait (1982)

In my conservatory (1983)

With my R.T.S. Award (1985)

At home in Southport

Hilda with 'Our Hilda' rose (1986)

My leaving party with the cast of *Coronation Street* (1987)

studio wardrobe for many years until it began to fall apart at the seams. Then the writers allowed Stan and Len Fairclough to give it to the kids for their bonfire on November 5th. I was shattered when it went – a bit of my past went with it . . .

At the beginning of 1964 I did another series for Rediffusion called *Badger's End*. It was about a country vet and a farming family who used his services. I was the farmer's wife and we had two children. Naturally, farm animals appeared in great profusion, but for some reason wild animals were brought in too. Graham Dangerfield provided them. I went out of my way to seek his company so that I could get into closer contact with the animals.

One week we had a cheetah in the studio, brought in a huge cage on wheels. He was a magnificent animal and I, with my love of cats of all sizes, was thrilled by him, going close to the cage and peering in, dying to touch him, attracted and repelled at the same time by his power and grace and by the fierce cruelty of his beautiful eyes. In the tea break on recording day I said to the cheetah's keeper, the owner of a private zoo, 'Can I stroke him?' expecting a flat refusal.

But he did not seem surprised at my request. 'Oh, yes, it'll be all right if you don't make any quick movements, just stroke him slowly. Put your hand in first and let him sniff it. As long as I'm here things won't go wrong.'

'Then please don't go away!' I said. I put my hand through the bars and stroked the animal's ears just as if I were stroking our old Mungo. The cheetah put his head on one side, tilted his chin to be stroked under-neath, again just like Mungo. Then he stopped purring and put his nose on my hand. It took all my courage not to jerk my hand away. Hello, here go my fingers, I thought. But no, apparently he wasn't hungry. He started to wash my hand, front, back and between the fingers almost up to my elbow. His great rasping tongue felt like a cheese grater. Now he's softening me up to enjoy a human arm, was my next thought, and by now I was getting a little nervous. So when he turned his head away I withdrew my hand quietly and steadily so as not to alarm him. Then I started to shake. The owner looked at me with some respect. 'Not many people would do that,' he said, 'but he's moderately tame so there was no real danger. You were wise not to irritate him.'

My rapport with cats was greatly increased by the episode; if I could take on a cheetah what next could I attempt? Then I thought of Albert and the Lion at Blackpool Zoo and decided that for the moment enough was enough.

On another occasion Graham Dangerfield brought an apricot-coloured mink to the studio, a really beautiful little creature. It was in a wooden box about three feet long, ten inches wide and eight inches high, with wire netting over the top. Apparently mink are terribly energetic, they rush around for five minutes or so then go into a coma. They flop down on their back with their paws in the air for about a minute and remain in a state of suspended animation, mouth open and little white teeth showing. Then up they get and resume their frantic running around as though seven devils were after them. 'I'd love to stroke its tummy,' I said to Graham.

'Have you noticed its teeth?' he said.

I looked. They were like a set of fine chisels. 'If you put your finger through that netting it would bite your finger down to the bone,' Graham warned. 'They are among the most vicious creatures alive,' and he showed me the thick leather gauntlets he wore when he had to take the mink from its cage. The actor playing the vet had to wear them too and he was heard to wonder why he had not stuck to selling insurance. So I never got to stroking a mink's coat until I wore my own champagne mink twenty years later.

In February, 1964 Joan phoned me. They were casting a new family in *Coronation Street* and she had an audition lined up for me. 'Oh, dear,' I said. 'People have told me hair-raising stories about working in a series; you get typecast and when you're out of the show you never work again.' The more I thought about it the more wary I became, but Joan was very patient with me. 'I don't know whether I really want to do it,' I went on. 'Whether it's for a few weeks or a few months, the end result might be a blight on my career.'

'You haven't got the job yet,' Joan said drily. 'There's no harm in going for the interview. Do that and see what happens.'

'Oh, all right,' I said ungraciously, 'though I'd rather work in London.'

The interview was at the Granada offices in Golden Square. There were two other interviewees while I was there. Hilary Mason was before me and Barbara Miller after me. I feel rather ashamed at being unable to remember who interviewed me and what questions they asked.

One of the interviewers said, doubtfully, 'You look rather young and smart for the part,' so I dived into my bag and pulled out a photograph of me dressed as Marty in *Anna Christie*, in the make-up that my own father had failed to penetrate. That provoked a favourable gasp, and I felt one up!

The interview over I went back to waiting for work and drawing the dole – for the next three months. In April I got a small part in *Mary Barton*, an adaptation of the Mrs Gaskell novel. This took me to Glasgow for three weeks and I had a very enjoyable time. Cyril Luckham, who sadly died in early 1989, was in the cast, and I told him that in my pre-theatre days I had often seen him at the Playhouse in Liverpool, where he spent many years. 'I could never master the Liverpool accent,' he admitted. 'Say something in Liverpool for me !' So I would give him a burst of pure Scouse, which he found highly amusing, and I had to perform my party piece (which was actually returning to my linguistic roots) every time we met. With *Mary Barton* in the can I returned to London at the end of April. Mum and dad, now happy again in Sefton Street, had arranged to go to Guernsey for a fortnight and asked me to go with them. I could just about manage to pay my share of the expenses so I agreed, and it was all very pleasant. We returned on a Saturday and mum and dad were to stay with me in Cromwell Road for a night. I opened the front door and was confronted by Michael, who said, 'There's been a telephone call for you. You have to go to Granada in Manchester on Monday. Something to do with *Coronation Street*.'

The next day I caught the coach to Southport with mum and dad and on Monday presented myself at the Granada studios, still feeling rather wary. I was not going to be pushed into anything I did not want to do.

I was briefly introduced to a large friendly man called Bernard Youens and to two boys who were being tried out for parts as the Ogden children, and we did a dry run; that is, we learned a little scene and recorded it. All I was rewarded with was, 'Thank you, we'll let you know.' Never had it taken so long to know whether or not I'd got a part, especially one that I was not too keen on! Nor was I quite sure what the part was all about if I were to get it – a nosy gossip with a slobbish husband was all I could gather from the short scene we had done. So I returned to London on Tuesday and heard nothing more till Friday. Then Joan rang. 'Back to Manchester next Monday,' she announced.

'Oh, *no!*' I groaned. 'Not again! What is it for this time?'

'Another dry run,' Joan said but could give me no further details.

Off I went again and did another scene with Bernard and with two different boys, then back to London on Tuesday where I forgot all about it till Friday, when I heard from Joan again. 'Right – *you're in!*' she said brightly.

So easily can one's future be determined . . . There was no further argument from me. I had to pack up, say goodbye to Michael and Charles and to all the friends I had in London and shoot up to Southport on Sunday ready for my debut the following day.

CHAPTER 14

'Street' Friends

I HAD never heard of Bernard Youens before meeting him at the dry run, nor had he heard of me. Bunny, as I grew to call him, was older than me and had been in the theatre before me. In the forties and fifties he had been a tall, dark, handsome leading man! In 1955 he became a continuity announcer for Granada, chosen for his cultured voice with its hint of sexiness. He was given the chance of an audition for a part in *Coronation Street* four years before he actually joined the cast but turned it down because, as a married man with five children, he did not care to risk the possibility of a short engagement that might soon leave him out of work. Bunny had known lean times, like so many of us in *The Street*. Before the war he had worked in various Reps, but things at one stage were so bad that he gave up the theatre altogether, became a publican, bread salesman and a labourer on a building site before the continuity job came up. When *Coronation Street* became such a long-running hit Bunny grabbed a second chance to audition, and the result was Stan Ogden.

The introduction of new characters to the programme was due to the 'great purge' of 1964. A new young producer called Tim Aspinall had the idea of shaking up a programme that he thought was getting too bland and cosy and whose ratings were slipping. The first character to go, quite arbitrarily, was Martha Longhurst, played by Lynne Carol. She was the nasty old gossip and crony of Ena Sharples and Minnie Caldwell. She was made to have a sudden heart attack, and she collapsed on the pub table and died. Other familiar faces to go were those of Frank Pemberton, Doreen Keogh and Ivan Beavis. It was all done in a very high-handed way and the actors resented the fact that the Press had the news of who was leaving before the actors themselves. But things cooled down and Bunny and I were given a friendly reception when we arrived. It was accepted that the unpopular changes had not been manipulated by us!

Bunny and I hit it off immediately. At the very first reading I thought, 'I know how this bloke works,' and he, it transpired, thought the same about me. We did not confide in each other that we both admired the other's approach until much later, but our rapport was evident from the outset. Our method was to know the lines thoroughly, play around with them, make sure that we knew what we wanted to do, then do it. We got to the point that we could rehearse our lines in a quiet corner, play Scrabble at the same time, and swear at each other when one or the other was making too high a score.

We played Scrabble for eight years then one day we stopped and never played again. We had got so good at it that we could block each other's moves after three or four turns so that neither of us was able to move a letter. There was no point in playing any more . . .

Being able to work with Bunny so easily was an amazing piece of good fortune for me. I gained so much more confidence than I would otherwise have done, and could feel at home in my part so much more quickly. The part of Hilda had been conceived as a nagging wife married to a fat lout, but both Bunny and I knew that the Ogdens would not last long if that was all they were going to be, and we worked hard to give them more depth, humour, a touch of pathos occasionally, and a deep bond between them that Stan's frequent lapses from commonsense could not shake. Hilda could criticise him as loud and long as she liked, and did, but she defended him furiously if anyone else cast aspersions on his character. There was always a sense of deep pride when she talked of 'my Stan', just as Stan's 'our 'ilda' contained a tinge of awe. Together they formed a solid alliance against a world that was out to do them down. Audiences laughed at their antics but also applauded their resilience, and their popularity grew rapidly.

The only member of the cast I had known before joining *The Street* was Eileen Derbyshire from Southport days, and it was like seeing a lamp in the darkness when we met again and had a good gossip about old times.

Eileen had started in the programme two months after it opened; she had to turn down the chance of a part when the first auditions were held because she was involved in a pantomime; but within six months she was on a regular contract and Miss Nugent, later Mrs Bishop, Mrs Swain and back to Mrs Bishop again, was in. The continuity was only broken twice, by a six months Equity strike, and when she left for a year to have a baby. So, apart from William Roache, she is the oldest surviving member of the original cast. And there is absolutely no similarity between Emily Bishop's personality and her own. She bubbles over with life and laughter is never very far from the surface even in her most harrowing scenes.

Everybody was extremely nice to me when I joined *The Street*. I was feeling somewhat apprehensive, wondering whether the old regulars would have much time for an unknown newcomer. Bernard knew them all because of his work as a staff announcer so he started on a rather different basis. But I need not have worried. As soon as they saw that I was serious about the job and behaved professionally, did not put on any airs and graces (why should I have done, anyway?) and was willing to be part of a team, I was taken to the collective hearts of Violet Carson, Margot Bryant, Doris Speed, Jack Howarth, Arthur Leslie and the others. I grew to be extremely fond of most of the cast and the more we worked together the more friendly we became. One or two earned my respect rather than my affection and it was probably my fault that we were not closer, but whatever my personal feelings were there was no doubt about my admiration for their abilities.

Margot Bryant was perhaps the most eccentric character and we got on well together because we both had a passion for cats, though I doubt whether I would have gone so far as to take tins of cat meat to Venice to feed the starving feline population there. As Minnie Caldwell she was dithering, a little slow, easily put upon, a soft pincushion of an old lady, but Margot Bryant was actually a very forceful character with an enormous vocabulary of obscenities. Well-dressed, elegant, dripping with jewellery, one could not imagine that pursed-up, lady-like mouth uttering such words. I had only been in the studio a couple of days when, opening the door of the Green Room, I heard a little Minnie Caldwell voice saying, 'And the car was so filthy I wrote F*** on the bonnet with my finger!' I could hardly believe my ears, 'Did Margot Bryant say that?' I asked somebody.

'You haven't heard the half of it!' I was told.

After Margot had been more than usually outrageous she would laugh so much that tears streamed from her eyes and she would be wiping them away for ten minutes afterwards. She was a very funny lady, but tough; a dragon lurked beneath her meek and mild exterior. She could not bear rudeness or inefficiency. Airline staff (she loved flying and would be off to New York for a Broadway opening at the drop of a hat) and British Rail officials often felt the rough edge of her tongue. Assistants in Kendal Milne's, the Harrod's of Manchester, used to hide under their counters when they saw her coming. They knew that if everything was not just right for her there would be sharp words and bitter complaints.

An actor friend once gave her a lift from Brighton, where she lived, to Manchester. They stopped off at a Forte service station for a coffee and a bun. Alas for them the bun was stale . . . In the afternoon when I arrived for rehearsal I found Margot writing furiously, the nib almost piercing the paper with the force of her feelings. 'I'm writing to Sir Charles Forte,' she said. 'His coffee was cold and his bun was stale.'

She received a reply by return. Through his secretary Sir Charles apologised and explained that as the incident had happened at ten o'clock on a Monday morning the first delivery of fresh buns had not been made, so the one she had been served with had been left over from Saturday. They would do their best to make an earlier delivery in future and he hoped that she would continue to patronise his café.

Margot was born in Hull, the daughter of a doctor who went on his rounds in a horse and trap. At the end of the last century the doctor was looked on as a sort of minor god, and Margot and her sister, who were educated privately at home, came to regard themselves as above the common herd. This snobbish attitude never quite left her. It is surprising that both she and her sister went into the theatre, at first on the musical side, and Margot understudied Adele Astaire in *Stop Flirting* and *Lady be Good*. She later turned legitimate and worked in theatres all over the country. Her introduction to *Coronation Street* was as an extra – an old lady who never said a word but submitted to Ena Sharples's withering comments on her intelligence. Then she was occasionally given the odd line which, in her inimitable way, she made funny; and so Minnie Caldwell became the character who earned so much sympathy from the viewers. What they did not know was Margot's ability to forget key words in her dialogue and substitute others that frequently made no sense. 'My father had a dog once,' she said. 'It was a ferret . . .'

Margot came to stay with me in Southport on more than one occasion. The first time was when I discovered that she was going to spend Christmas on her own in her little flat in Manchester because we were working on both sides of Christmas, which fell at the weekend. She would not have had time to go to her Brighton flat so when I asked her home to Southport she said, 'Oh, lovely,' and arrived with three bottles of champagne. We had a marvellous weekend.

Margot, whose life was dominated by cats even more than mine was (when Eileen Derbyshire was showing her new baby around Margot's comment was, 'What a pity it isn't a kitten!'), was like a cat herself. She could purr and she could scratch. She had to be warm and all the Christmas weekend our house was like a furnace. Even though she wore a heavy woollen dress and shawl she sat huddled over the fire the whole time. The house positively *bulged* with heat and mother and I had to keep rushing out into the garden to cool down. The following year she stayed with us again at Christmas, and then came an Easter visit. We took her to Marion's for a drink and there she sat regally in the best chair in fur coat, fur hat, shawl and gloves, clutching her double brandy.

In spite of their totally different backgrounds she and mother got on very well. Mother was not the sort of person to be intimidated by grandness and Margot wisely treated her as though they had been girls together. I gave them both full marks for trying.

Margot's relationship with Violet Carson was all it should be. They were professionals who knew that the job came first and that any differences in temperament had to be left outside the studio. Violet was a super person. She was outspoken too and had no inhibitions about giving her opinion when something displeased her, but she was never rude or discourteous. Even in fierce arguments she was polite, blunt in a typically Northern way, but straightforward. You knew where you were with Violet. She could give the impression of being intimidating, and newcomers to the cast would be a bit wary of her. But when they got to know her better they realised that they need not have been scared; and certainly the regular members of the company felt only affection for her and were bowled over by her charm. If you took a pride in your work and did not show off Violet took you into her circle.

In the early days she and Arthur Leslie used to travel to Blackpool, where they both lived, every night after rehearsals or recordings. I went to Southport so we three would share a taxi to the station, and it was then that I first realised what a lovely person Vi was. Later she stayed at the Midland Hotel during the week, only going home at the weekend. On Thursday nights I would sometimes stay there too, and we would meet in the bar for a drink and a chat. Everybody in the hotel thought the world of her, which speaks volumes.

I once returned to the rehearsal room early after lunch and was just about to open the door when I heard someone playing the piano that had been brought in for a scene with Ena Sharples. It was Violet playing some Schubert and then Chopin's 'Raindrop Prelude'. I stood there for several minutes, entranced. She had a magic touch, her fingers were like feathers, which was strange because her hands were square and podgy. But there was power behind the lightness. A lot of people remember her playing the piano in the radio show *Have a Go* with Wilfred Pickles but few realised just how accomplished a pianist she was.

It was common knowledge that I did not like Pat Phoenix; indeed, Pat mentioned it in her autobiography. Everybody accepted the fact that we were chalk and cheese and that it was impossible for us to get on together – but the odd thing is that it simply was not true! Pat and I became entangled in a great misunderstanding, and it got to the point when, if she saw Tony Warren, the originator of *Coronation Street*, talking to me she would hiss 'Traitor!' to him as she stalked by. In the end we were sensible enough to sort things out to our mutual satisfaction, discovered that we *did* like and respect each other and stayed liking each other until her untimely death in 1986.

It all arose from my shyness and Pat's flamboyance. I never knew what to say to her! There are people I can meet for the first time and talk to as though I have known them for years, and others make me completely tongue-tied because I cannot find a point of contact with them. Pat was one of the latter. All the time we were in the show together we never had a proper conversation. The things that she was interested in were beyond my range, and I don't suppose she thought a lot about my gardening activities or my love of music. For years if I was left alone in the Green Room with her there would be an embarrassed silence and I would think, 'What *can* I talk about...?' and I could not think of a thing.

Pat was something beyond my ken. Extrovert, brassy, loud, good-natured, generous to a fault – Hollywood in Lancashire! She had a wide circle of friends and a social life that the Queen might have envied. By contrast I went back to my semi in Southport every night and put my feet up. Nobody ever attempted to drink champagne out of *my* shoe! Things went from bad to worse and we were each convinced that each hated the other, when in fact Pat did not have the temperament to hate anybody, and neither had I.

When she was about to get married to Alan Browning, who played her husband in *The Street*, she was not going to invite me to the wedding. But Alan, whom I *could* talk to, said, 'You *must* invite Jean,' and Pat grudgingly gave in. So I went to the wedding, keeping well in the background. For a wedding present I gave her a silver tray for her pre-breakfast cup of tea, something I had heard she had always wanted. That did it. All imaginary hatchets were buried, there was a touching reunion and Pat and Jean were friends from then on, to everybody's relief.

Anne Reid and William Roache were two other people I found it hard to talk to, though there was never any feud, imaginary or otherwise, between us. I liked them both very much and admired their talent, but as for chatting inconsequentially, as I could with so many of the other actors, I always felt inhibited. In 23 years my conversations with Bill were limited to, 'Hello', 'What a terrible day,' 'Isn't it hot?' and, 'Have you got a lot to do next week?' Bill was interested in esoteric religions, philosophy, the deep things of life – when he was not buying, restoring and selling old houses or leading a card school in the Green Room – and my butterfly mind was not up to his level when it came to exploring the universe. I was always a somewhat naturally reserved person and not the greatest chatterer in the world, and I am sure that on occasion I have given the impression of being indifferent to or antagonistic towards people I secretly look up to; but with my special friends I can natter for hours and not repeat myself. Being human is a terrible burden!

One of the most respected actors in *The Street* was Jack Howarth, a professional to his finger tips. He always knew his lines, never let a fellow actor down, was aware of the exact effect he was creating, pathetic or funny. It was a joy to work with him.

Before joining *Coronation Street* Jack had been 14 years as Mr Maggs in *Mrs Dale's Diary*, the radio serial, and before that he had had a lifetime of experience in the theatre – from 1908 when he was 12 years old. When he became Albert Tatlock there was quite a heated debate among the production team as to whether or not the character should have a moustache. Jack thought that he should and won the argument. But the bushy little moustache above his upper lip was false and was applied before every recording. Asked why he did not grow a real one and save the make-up girl the bother of putting it on he replied that his wife would not fancy him with one.

Out of the scores of superb scenes in which Jack showed his great talent I think that the funniest was the one in which he and Jack Walker of the *Rovers Return* had been to a 'do' at the British Legion and had finished up drunk as lords. When Jack got home to the pub Annie Walker tore him off a strip while Albert, waiting at a bus stop, gradually slid down a lamp post till he was sitting on the ground, bowler hat over one eye, singing *If I Ruled the World*. The scene could hardly be filmed for the laughter that came from the onlookers.

Jack Howarth was inordinately fond of Eccles cakes, a great Northern delicacy (the South provides only a pale imitation). During rehearsals a trolley would appear at the tea break to save us having to go down to the canteen. It contained the usual things: tea, coffee, biscuits, buns, cakes – and Eccles cakes. Jack was always first at the trolley and the Eccles cakes disappeared like lightning, one in each hand and one in each pocket.

On recording days we did a sort of dress rehearsal and then repaired to a side room where refreshments were laid out and where the producer would give us notes and get us prepared for the actual recording. Again Jack was always first into the room, trundling along on his little legs like a Puffing Billy. One day Bunny and I, having finished our scene before the others, looked through the glass doors and saw Jack taking the cling film from every plate of cakes and whipping away all the Eccles cakes. Then he put the transparent cover back. He did not know that we had seen him and when we arrived at the table he straightened up, looked at me (knowing that I liked Eccles cakes too) and said, with the most innocent expression in the world, 'Er, there's an Eccles cake here, you'd better take it before the others come.' And he already had about six in his pockets. He was like an endearing little hamster.

For Jack's 80th birthday Geoff Bentley, the scenic artist, was asked to make a birthday cake that wasn't exactly a cake. He made a big wooden tray, decorated it beautifully, and made the figures '80' in rings of Eccles cakes; he put a candle in each circle of the '8' and another in the 'o', and in the tea break he brought it into the studio and presented it to Jack. Jack had a very gruff exterior, very like that of the character he played, and he could chunter away Albert Tatlock-like to the life, but he was really an emotional old gentleman. When he saw his birthday tribute his face crumpled up and there were tears in his eyes. We made him blow out the candles, then when we had each taken a cake he was allowed to take the rest home. He swore it was the best birthday present he had ever had.

Doris Speed was another member of the cast who was a real 'character'. She had been in *The Street* from the first episode; indeed, Tony Warren, who wrote it, had Doris in mind for the publican's wife even before he had written a single word. Over the years she either took over the character of Annie Walker or Annie took over Doris. I don't know which, but at times it was impossible to know who was who. She could put on the airs of a grand lady but she had a lovely dry wit and told endless stories against herself. She lived with her widowed mother Ada, a very old lady who had been in the theatre and was an ardent *Coronation Street* fan. Doris once had a very long emotional scene into which she put her whole heart, finishing with a flood of tears. She made it very affecting and we, watching, were full of admiration for her performance.

The following week when it was transmitted Doris was watching it with her mother, and when the credits went up she sat very still, hoping for a word of praise from the old lady. 'Well, mother,' she said eventually, thinking that perhaps her mother was too moved to speak.

'Was that your own apron, Doris?' her mother said, 'or was it from wardrobe?'

Doris was very politically minded, a keen Socialist. She played bridge like a professional and went through crossword puzzles like a knife through butter. Sometimes, *Guardian* in hand, she would say to me, if she was temporarily stuck for an answer, 'You're clever, dear, what is No. 17 down?' and once or twice by sheer luck I got the answer. Afterwards Doris treated me as a fellow intellectual, which was very embarrassing!

Though Doris could be a bit grand she was a warm and humorous person beneath the façade. She hated handling props, they distracted her, and if she had to pour out a cup of tea and speak her lines at the same time she could dry completely. Once she cleared all the ashtrays from the bar of the *Rovers Return* just before we were about to record a scene. They were my props. I was going to empty them and polish them with a duster to give me something to do. It had all been rehearsed. Waiting to start the scene I suddenly noticed that the counter was bare and I felt a moment of panic. 'Where have all my props gone? Doris, have you seen my ashtrays and duster?'

'Oh,' said Doris, 'they're under the counter. I don't like things like that in front of me while I'm working.'

'But, Doris, I *use* them,' I spluttered.

'Do you, dear?' she said vaguely.

'Yes, I do. I've been rehearsing with them all week!' So she had to fish them all out again and put them on the bar just in time. Dear Doris, she was quite oblivious to anything going on that was not connected with Annie Walker and what Annie was saying. Her famous upward look into the middle distance was simply put on to prevent her from being distracted by another actor's reaction.

Doris was much older than any of us thought. She is as old as the century, I believe, but she pretended to be a good 15 years younger.

When she was suddenly taken ill and had to leave the programme we were all devastated, and we worried about her long period of depression that followed. We were relieved to learn that her affairs were eventually taken over by Granada, who sorted out her finances, sold her house and established her in a home where she could be properly looked after. Now she is as spry as ever, playing bridge with her cronies and holding court as though she were still the gracious landlady of the *Rovers Return*.

Barbara Knox, who joined the cast in 1972, is one of the finest actresses that *The Street* has ever had. There is a quality about her work that puts her among the best of modern actresses. She is superb in both comedy and tragedy. She has a wonderful deadpan throwaway technique, with a look or a twist of the lips that can say more than a long speech. The way she handles dialogue is masterly and she has given the programme some of the most moving scenes it has ever had. Her reaction to Len Fairclough's death, for instance, her pleading to Alan Bradley to return to her, and her devastation when she finally realises how he has used her: if ever an actress deserves some kind of official recognition it is Barbara Knox.

In real life she is charming and witty when she is willing to reveal herself, but essentially she is a very private person, having made a sensible decision never to give interviews to the Press. I wish sometimes that I had done the same. Actually I have given very few, but many articles have appeared in which I have seemed to lay the law down about a number of subjects when, in fact, I have never seen the interviewer at all! Everything has been made up. One can only shrug one's shoulders and laugh it off.

Barbara's career has been similar to mine in some ways. She has acted at Oldham and at York, though some years after I was there, and she shares my opinion of Donald Bodley as a great producer. Her experience also includes TV series and radio.

Barbara Knox and Thelma Barlow are universally acknowledged to be one of the funniest double acts ever to appear in a series. When a scene starts with cynical Rita and twittering Mavis in the *Kabin* millions of viewers sit back and prepare to be entertained. Barbara and Thelma are good friends, they spark each other off as people and their compatibility is reflected in their acting. Their timing is impeccable. Each knows exactly how the other is going to react, and what the reaction to the reaction is going to be. Neither tries to outdo the other, they both set an example of generous acting. Rehearsals of their scenes were always hugely enjoyable for the rest of us.

It is well known that Thelma Barlow is the exact antithesis of Mavis Riley, that she is highly competent at everything she sets out to do, whether it is gardening, cookery or sewing, that she knows about herbs and wine, and is interested in serious drama. From Joan Littlewood's Theatre Workshop in London she went on to Rep in Bristol, Nottingham and Glasgow and parts in West End productions. Mavis in real life would drive Thelma up the wall, and Thelma drives me to despair because she is so bright, positive, intelligent and articulate!

Peter Adamson was a person I once respected but he was his own worst enemy, one of the best actors in *The Street* and one of the saddest. On his good days he was funny and generous, on others he was argumentative and aggressive. He treated his alcohol problem with great courage and, having won his battle over ten years, worked hard for fellow sufferers. His career on the programme had been almost cut short several times due to drunken brawls and fights with Granada, though it was eventually severed when the Press got hold of him. For a large sum of money they persuaded him to 'tell all' about his fellow actors, including those who had supported him and tried to cover up the increasing inadequacy of his performances; hurtful and untrue allegations that the Peter Adamson we had once known would not have made. I was lucky to come out of it unscathed though he did give away a secret we shared that I would have preferred not to be publicised.

In 1983 Granada did not renew his contract. He went into the theatre, then to Canada for a while to rebuild his acting career. I thought at one time that Peter was more sinned against than sinning and that the way he wrecked his private life was a matter for sympathy, but his disloyalty to his friends made it hard to forgive him.

During my years in *The Street* so many characters walked along its cobblestones, leaned on the bar of the *Rovers Return*, fought, married and died. Some stayed, some left, some made a lasting impression, others faded from memory quickly. Most of them were easy to get on with, good at their work and an asset to the programme. Only a few were total misfits, big-headed, arrogant, unable to take direction, and they were soon gladly forgotten.

I have mentioned some of the great names of the past, and some of the present, and if I skirt over the lives and characters of other friends it is only for reasons of space, not because I do not admire their work or value the support they gave me. Johnny Briggs, for instance, ex-boy soprano, who is no hustler from Bermondsey and male chauvinist in real life but a sportsman who works hard for charity; and he is also an actor who is so easy to work with because he *gives*. Anne Kirkbride goes from strength to strength; she achieved an acting triumph when she was part of the love tangle between Deirdre, husband Ken and Mike Baldwin, and they received special recognition at the Pye Television Awards.

William Tarmey, the leering opportunist, Jack Duckworth, whose money-making schemes, like Stan's, inevitably end in disaster, is a former cabaret singer and TV extra, and is devoted to his real wife. Elizabeth Dawn, as Vera Duckworth, is as funny off screen as she is on. She has a heart as big as Vera's voice is loud, and she too works incessantly for charity. She is also a cabaret singer and experienced in many aspects of show business. Roy Barraclough is one of the most experienced actors ever to appear on *The Street*. Nothing like his rather sleazy persona as Alec Gilroy, he has worked with many famous names, particularly Les Dawson. Ada and Cissie, two garrulous and grotesque 'ladies' of a certain age and less certain pasts, will never be forgotten. It was a pleasure to work with Roy; easy, genial, and so professional it was like being supported by a rotund life jacket!

Julie Goodyear is another person it is good to work with. Although her private life has been a soap opera in itself she has always bounced back, earrings swinging bravely. She has survived cervical cancer, raised money for a screening laboratory, and has faced a sometimes hostile world with a defiant shrug. She is rock-steady in performance, always word perfect and never makes a wrong move.

Jill Summers, the blue-rinsed, man-mad Phyllis Pearce, who has spent more than 70 years in show business, among other things as a stand-up comedienne, joined *Coronation Street* in 1982. She is famous for her reply to a flasher who opened his raincoat to her one dark night as she was going to the station. 'Eee,' she said, taking it all in, 'you *are* a sport!' Collapse of flasher, who was not used to that kind of reaction.

Sue Nicholls is another wonderful colleague. As Audrey Roberts she is flighty, extravagant, squawky-voiced, and has been no better than she should be. Off screen Sue is elegant, well-spoken (well, she has a County background and went to a posh school), and is surprisingly unambitious. She had a period of ill-health, dealt with in the plot by sending her to Canada to nurse a son whom Gail never knew existed, and everybody was very pleased when she returned to the programme fit and well.

Bill Waddington, the pompous know-all, Percy Sugden, is another oldtimer in show business whose career goes back more than 40 years. He tends to gather round him the former veteran music-hall per-formers in the cast, and they swap stories of 'the time when' variety. Percy's character is on the whole one-dimensional but there are times when Bill can bring a moment of pathos to the usually bombastic lollipop man. It is interesting to speculate how he would have got on with Ena Sharples!

Christopher Quinten asked to have his contract terminated when he married an American and went to Hollywood to seek fame and fortune and was, as Brian Tilsley, knifed to death in a street brawl. That's what happens in *Coronation Street* when the producers have no intention of letting you return – you get bumped off! Christopher was a very brash young man when he joined us and his acting ability was not notable for its depth or flexibility, but in the ten years he played the swaggering young garage-owner he improved greatly, supported by Helen Worth, Lynn Perrie and others who worked with him and taught him the importance of team work. I once had to take him aside and talk to him like a Dutch aunt about his attitude to his work. He took it like a lamb – after sulking for four days ... Helen Worth, his wife Gail, has hair the colour of honey, and a nature to match, sweet and golden. She is a shy girl, a private person who never puts on airs, and is as delightful an actress as she is a person.

Lynne Perrie has spent a lifetime in show business, including cabaret all over the world. She is a real 'trouper' who brings great gusto to the part of Ivy Tilsley. As Ivy she can be prejudiced, bossy, argumentative and unforgiving, but Lynne can express a more human and sentimental side with great tenderness. Her reconciliation with Gail after Brian's death was particularly moving.

Geoffrey Hughes as Eddie Yeats dovetailed in perfectly with Bernard and me; our comedy duo became a trio with perfect ease. He came into the programme in 1974, on parole from Walton gaol (Eddie, not Geoffrey!), and quickly established himself as the likeable, fat, gap-toothed binman. Stan and Hilda looked upon him as another, and favourite, son and he brightened their lives with his dodgy schemes and heart of gold. Geoffrey left the programme to explore new acting opportunities and we were very sorry to see him go. He made a brief re-appearance to see Hilda in hospital in 1987 and was offered a long term contract. It was our loss when he declined. He and I were on the same wavelength every step of the way.

There are some extremely talented young people in *The Street* nowadays who are replacing those of us who have left or died, and the programme will never lose its relevance or its popularity while they are giving such convincing performances. Sally Ann Matthews, Sally Whittaker, Michael Le Vell, Kevin Kennedy, Lisa Lewis and Sean Wilson: *The Street* is safe in their hands, and they deserve grateful thanks from the bosses at Granada!

And last, but not least, Betty Driver – dear Betty, my very best friend in *The Street* for nearly 20 years. The kindly, sharp-tongued, down to earth barmaid famed for her hotpot lunches, the fictional Betty Turpin is not too far removed from the real Betty, the sort of person to whom one can tell one's deepest secrets and know that they will be firmly locked in that capacious bosom for ever.

Betty has had an amazing career – radio, West End theatre, records, films and TV. She was a child star when she was 14, sang for seven years with Henry Hall, appeared in some of the early Ealing comedies, and toured the world entertaining the troops during the Second World War. Utterly reliable as a *Street* actress, utterly loyal as a person, she has a heart as big as Buckingham Palace. She and I used to sit in the dressing-room when we had free time and make padded coat-hangers with colourful materials and sell them for our pet charity, the Angioscope Fund of Queen Elizabeth's Hospital in Birmingham. We also made personal appearances for the same charity. We made thousands of coat-hangers and sold them for £1 each. I'm sure our friends in the cast have wardrobes full of our product but they were always very good when another batch was brought out for sale.

Betty has a remarkable ability to provide the perfect description of something she is telling you about: similes pop out with picturesque abandon. A baby owl that had got blown out of a shed looked like 'a tawny chrysanthemum', and 'a walnut on legs' was how she described a little wren she saw sitting on her window sill; and of a baggy-trousered farmer she said, 'You know, he looked as if he'd got five pounds of King Edwards in the arse of his trousers.' Her sense of humour is as unpredictable as Eileen's or mine, with an added saltiness.

When Betty Turpin's husband Cyril died she was, naturally, heart-broken. Annie Walker, Bet Lynch, Emily Bishop and Alf Roberts all called at her house to wait for the car that would take them to the cemetery for the funeral and were ushered into the front room. They were all dressed in black and wore suitably lugubrious expressions. They sat around stiffly while Betty went upstairs to get her coat. Suddenly there came floating downstairs an anguished cry like a constipated owl. 'Cy-ril! Cy-ril!' The four mourners collapsed with sudden helpless mirth. 'Cy-ril!' came another hoot and they, and we who were watching the rehearsal, were almost rolling on the floor. Betty appeared at the top of the stairs, saw what was happening and had to grip the banisters to steady herself. The director had to start the scene from the beginning four times before there was enough composure to get through the take.

All the funerals in *The Street* took place in the same disused Manchester cemetery, and the same hole was used to lower the coffin in. Each funeral was filmed from a different angle to make it look authentic and each one gave rise to scarcely controlled hysteria as the empty coffin was reverently let down. Ernie Bishop's funeral was the most difficult the mourners ever had to cope with. The butty wagon was standing nearby, serving tea, coffee, sandwiches and suchlike. It was a very cold morning for the filming and business at the van was brisk. Just as the coffin disappeared from view and Emily Bishop was looking suitably ravaged she happened to look up and saw a figure appear from behind a gravestone, out of camera range, with a bacon butty in his hand. It was the dead Ernie Bishop, supposedly in the coffin – Stephen Hancock, who had come to see his own 'funeral'. It does not take much to set Eileen going, and another group of mourners became limp with laughter. Every time they tried to get back into character they saw Stephen chewing his sandwich and a sudden heaving of funereal shoulders would set the rest off again. Would that all funerals were such jolly affairs!

CHAPTER 15

Stan and Hilda

STAN and Hilda had many moments of comedy that were not written in the script; one of the most bizarre was the 'waking-up machine'. Stan got a job as a milkman and had to start his early round at four o'clock in the morning. He always had a problem with waking up, so Hilda made him sleep in the living-room on a sofa so that the machine he had devised would be really effective. This device had actually been built by Chris McMaster, then the director.

First an ordinary alarm clock went off. It was standing in a tin dish so that the vibrations would be really loud. The alarm worked a string which set the radio going at full blast, and the radio activated a bowl of steel ball bearings which tipped up, sending them sliding down a chute and banging into another tin bowl on the table near to Stan's ear. It was all worked by different strings, I'm not quite sure of the mechanics, and the terrifying thing was that all this had to happen when the show was recorded as though it were live. There could be no breaks except for the advertisements and everything would have to stand. There could be no repeat if anything went wrong. Once the first string was cut everything depended on luck (and the director's skill). The contraption was set up at the beginning of the scene and there it stood . . . with us hoping that it would go right first time.

The alarm clock duly set off the radio and the Prelude to Act Three of Wagner's *Lohengrin* filled the studio. So far so good. At each musical climax somebody in the street was supposed to be awakened by the noise. Bedrooms had been built all round the studio and John Allen, the floor manager, was in turn cueing Ena Sharples, Minnie Caldwell,

Ken and Valerie Barlow, Jack and Annie Walker to shoot up in bed and say, 'What was that?' He did it by tweaking their toes.

The only person who did not wake up was, of course, Stan. Radio, ball bearings – nothing roused him. Hilda and Irma, their daughter, came running down the stairs, shouting things like, 'Wake up, you fat-headed chump!' and, 'Get up, you big lummock!' Stan slept on, the neighbours complained, Wagner bellowed forth, there was well-organised and well-rehearsed pandemonium, but nobody realised that the ball bearings that were falling down the chute into the tin were on impact immediately bouncing out again and falling all over the floor. The big camera of those early days was moving around the set, and it would have been jammed and prevented from moving if one of the ball bearings had got stuck underneath. So the floor manager, having done his cueing, had to duck down and crawl around, out of vision, to retrieve the ball bearings and stuff them into his pocket, getting redder and redder in the face through the unaccustomed exertion and the impulse to laugh out loud. Sandra Gough and I gallantly continued to play our parts, yelling at Stan and at each other as we tried not to see John Allen under the table with a fist full of ball bearings, Stan still snoring on the sofa, and Bunny not daring to open his eyes to see what was going on. We were all shattered at the end of the scene, but Chris McMaster in the control room kept amazingly cool – confident that his 'waking-up machine' had done its job as planned, not knowing what panic it had caused.

One Easter the scriptwriters decided that Bunny and I should go off for a weekend on a tandem – but, of course, nobody thought to ask us if we could ride one. We couldn't, though as a small child I rode an ordinary bicycle with all the panache I had gained at Rhyl. When we arrived at the studio on Monday morning for location work we found that we had been provided with a rickety, clapped-out machine with no grips on the handlebars, no pedals, only the spikes they should have fitted on, and covered with rust. Every time the wheels turned the chain fell off and the tyres were almost non-existent ... and we were expected to ride this moth-eaten contraption down the cobbles of *Coronation Street* then all the way to Deansgate Station where it was supposed to be put on a train.

Bunny weighed about 15 stone at the time, and I was eight stone four wet through. He was at the front and I was at the back, and it is the one at the back who does all the pushing while the front one has an easy ride. There was no way I could transport us both on that tandem, even if it had had all its parts working. In the end they had to film us from a three-quarter length angle, taking care not to show our feet. We pushed off each with one foot on the pavement, moved the bike a couple of yards with our feet on the ground, and we were next seen wheeling it into the station yard. The viewers were under the impression that we had ridden it expertly through the streets, though they had never actually seen us in action. Bunny and I agreed that the next time we had to use a machine we would inspect it carefully beforehand.

Stan and Hilda once heard a curious rustling noise which seemed to be coming from somewhere in the roof: it turned out to be pigeons roosting in the loft. The birds were supposed to fly down into the Ogden's bedroom below and land on the bed, but of course they did not know they had to follow the director's orders and flew around haphazardly all around the bedroom; the bed was the only place they ignored. Hilda climbed up into the loft to discover how the pigeons got in and there being no partition between the lofts of the two houses she found more birds in Elsie Tanner's loft too. She immediately blamed Elsie for the invasion and a big row ensued, Elsie in her bedroom and Hilda up above, trying to bash her way through the ceiling to prove her point. The set had been built with the ceiling about nine feet above the ground and I had been told just where to stamp so that my foot would come through and I could shout, 'There you are, Elsie Tanner, I told you they were in *your* loft!' The ceiling was meant to be made of cardboard just plastered lightly underneath, and I accepted the floor manager's word when he told me that my foot would break it easily. But what he did not know was that by mistake the ceiling had been made of solid wood, so when I stamped my foot I jarred every bone in my body, and a pain leapt right up into my head. I was sure that my five feet four inches would lack the four inches from then on. To make matters worse, being so far above the ground level, my vertigo was working overtime too. It was not a happy morning and when the scene was repeated, with a cardboard ceiling, the bad temper I had to register did not require any acting... Poor Elsie Tanner received more than she had expected.

Sometimes we went out of the studio for location filming, always a risky business in our climate, and usually we went to Salford. The first time I remember Bunny and me being on location was when Stan got a job with an ice cream van. Hilda decided that he needed her help so she went around with him. At one point she left the van and Stan took off in it, not realising she was not on board. 'Hey, Stan,' she cried in her high-pitched yelp, 'Wait for me! Stan – wait!' and she began to run along the cobbled street after the disappearing van. Real cobbles they were, and I had not come adequately prepared as I was wearing thin-soled winkle-pickers. They may have been fashionable but it was agony to run in them. We rehearsed the scene half a dozen times and my shoes became more and more vulnerable to the cobbles that seemed to be turning into razors. On top of that we did three takes because the camera had to keep moving to follow us and it also tended to rebel at the undulating road surface.

All in all I must have run up and down that street about ten times while Stan sat comfortably in the driving seat of the ice cream van. In the end I tottered back to the director and showed him my almost soleless and heelless shoes, my poor feet nearly through to the ankles. It was one of those times when I wondered was it worth it. Did the show *really* have to go on?

Another day on location had a happier result. It was at the time when Hilda suspected Stan of carrying on with ''er at 19, Inkerman Street', and made it her business to follow him, hoping to catch him red-handed in his illicit amour. It turned out that it was not the notorious woman in Inkerman Street that Stan was seeing, but an old lady who used to give him breakfast when he was on his milk round. I had to lurk round street corners and hide in entries, and we used little Salford streets. At one point Stan had to be filmed going into a house, and for some reason setting up the shot was proving difficult. I was not wanted until things had been sorted out so I stood in the doorway of a small terraced house, trying to keep warm. Suddenly the door opened behind me and an old gentleman stood there, ''Allo, love,' he said. 'It's a nasty morning – would you like a nice cup of tea?'

I glanced around. Nobody was watching me. 'I'd love one,' I said.

'Come in then,' he said and I followed him into the parlour. I was surprised to see a large policeman sitting there, helmet in his lap and a steaming mug in his hand. 'Hello, miss,' he said, and I realised that it was the policeman who was always on hand when we were on location filming. We had to have a policeman present to prevent trouble with onlookers or persistent fans.

The old man produced another mug and I took a sip. My eyes nearly popped out of my head and I spluttered. The tea was so well laced with whisky that it was difficult to tell which there was most of. The policeman was looking a bit glassy-eyed too. But by treating my drink as something lethal I was able to get it down eventually, and I appreciated the old gentleman's gesture – which was typical of Salford people. The remainder of my morning's filming turned out to be much more pleasant than I had anticipated due to my unexpected central heating.

Perhaps the most frightening story connected with my role as Hilda was that of the organ-grinder's monkey. I can't remember the story line but for some reason Stan came home one day with a small marmoset, very pretty but quite vicious. While we were rehearsing the scene the monkey was brought on in a cage, and to judge by the shrieks and the spitting it did not like it one bit. It flung itself around, banging on the bars and screaming so loudly that we could hardly make ourselves heard, and Bunny had to hold the cage firmly or it would have toppled off the table.

For the actual take Bunny had to carry the creature itself, not the cage. When the monkey had calmed down, the lights on and the camera running, we began. Bunny opened the door of the set, the monkey in his arms, and at that precise moment it bit him, hard. Bunny let out a yell and hurled the creature away from him. The tape was stopped. The monkey grinned. Bunny had to go for a tetanus injection and have his finger bandaged. When he returned he said with unaccustomed firmness, 'I'm not carrying that little swine on again. I'll bring it on in the cage or not at all. It's him or me!' The director agreed and the scene was shot without further complications.

We broke for tea. I needed to check my props for the next scene so I returned to the set early. To my surprise the monkey was out of its cage, its owner allowing it to cavort around the studio on a lead while we were all away. When it saw me it jerked away from the man and pulled the lead from his hand. I started to back away but it leapt on to the table then on to my shoulder. Before I took in what was happening the creature began to wrench the curlers out of my hair, pulling it as it did so. 'Get him off!' I shrieked, feeling the sharp claws twisting the curlers and scratching my scalp. I was not so much concerned with the curlers as with my eyes. The monkey's owner just stood there, and he was *laughing*. 'Eeh, just look at 'im! 'E does that to the wife, you know, takes 'er curlers out! Must like curlers, eh?' He gave another guffaw.

'You daft bugger,' I cried. 'Will you get him away . . . he'll scratch my eyes out!'

At that moment one of the camera boys arrived and saw the trouble I was in. 'Please,' I begged him. 'Please help me!' My eyes were closed tightly, there were no curlers left in my hair, my head was throbbing with pain. I don't usually cry, but I was near to it on that occasion.

The Good Samaritan quickly came to my rescue and somehow removed the horrid little beast from my head, taking no thought for his own safety.

The monkey's owner continued to look on, still laughing. ''E must have taken a right fancy to you. The wife'll be tickled pink when I tell 'er.'

I shall draw a discreet veil over what I said to him.

I suppose the most talked-about episode that Bunny and I were in was the one we called the 'Honeymoon Hotel' story, in November, 1977. It was very well written and really gave us something to get our teeth into, it being the first time we were taken out of our Ogden environment, away from No. 13, the pub and *Coronation Street* itself. Hilda had won a competition organised by Loving Cup Shandy with a slogan she invented: 'Be a mistress as well as a wife and your husband will always be your boy friend'. Strange words, coming from Hilda! The prize was a Second Honeymoon, a weekend in a four star hotel with the best of everything free.

The Piccadilly Hotel in Manchester was used to film us going through the doors into the foyer and up in the lift to Room 504, but the apartment we stayed in was actually built in the studio. There was a cocktail cabinet full of miniature bottles of every drink one could think of, and of course Stan sampled the lot besides swigging the free champagne. Hilda, in a seventh heaven of delight at the luxury surrounding her, sang *Room 504* in her high quavering voice, longing for a romantic response from Stan. But he was almost asleep, befuddled by drink, and when Hilda reached the last line of the song and gave him a wistful look a slurred voice said, 'Shurrup!' It was Bunny, putting in his own unscripted line, a piece of inspired improvisation that made a perfect ending to a sad little comedy.

My devotion to cats large and small has survived some bad experiences, but there was one occasion when my affection was sorely tested. It was possibly the most grotesque thing that has ever happened to me, and I shudder when the incident pops into my mind. It happened at the Belle Vue Zoo in Manchester where the cast had been taken by *TV Times* for photographs to celebrate the 10th anniversary of the programme. Betty Driver and I automatically found ourselves outside the tiger's cage. We stood there almost speechless with admiration of the magnificent animal, burning as brightly as Blake's tiger. The tiger looked at us with a serious expression on its intelligent face, mouth slightly open as though it were about to speak. 'Betty, I wonder what it's thinking about us,' I said.

Quickly, yet almost calculatedly, the tiger turned round, placed its rear against the bars of the cage and directed a jet of pungent liquid at us. Betty, not in a direct line, dodged to one side, but I, silly besotted me, stood immobile and was drenched from head to foot. With a toss of its head the tiger walked away, and I could have sworn I saw an expression of amusement on its face. I stood, face screwed up, mewing piteously. The others rushed up with tissues and handkerchiefs and I was partially dried; then a keeper arrived with a mopping-up cloth. But I stank of tiger and in the coach back to the studio I had to sit at the back, miserable and alone . . .

My long sojourn in TV was broken only once and that was due to a bit of conniving on the part of Bill Roache and Bunny. All casual-like Bill said to me one day, 'Jean, what's your favourite play?' Without thinking I said, *'Arsenic and Old Lace'*, which I knew well, having done it twice in Rep. 'Right,' said Bill and went away. Some time later he told me that he and Bunny were putting the play on at Oldham for a week, and they wanted me to be in it as one of the murderous sisters. The Oldham Theatre had been closed for three months for alterations and they wanted to re-open with a splash and have some locally well-known names in the cast.

I agreed reluctantly. I had not been on the stage for about 15 years and I did not know how I would be able to cope. I was terrified in rehearsal and similarly afflicted every night of the run. At the opening the theatre was packed to the rafters and it was the same every night of the week, so the run was extended for two more weeks. I didn't seem to be able to conquer my nerves, my ulcer played me up in the most unfriendly way. I lived on dry toast and milk and lost pounds. To make matters worse Granada had allowed us only one week off so for the two weeks the play was extended we were working during the day and had to rush off to Oldham every evening.

On Friday nights we did not finish recording until 6.30 p.m. and the curtain at Oldham went up at 7.30 p.m. One night Bill and I were kept waiting until the dot of 6.30 p.m.; Bunny and Brian Mosley, who was also in the cast, had got off early and gone on ahead. By the time Bill and I had cleaned up and changed it was a quarter to seven. We drove to Oldham in Bill's car in 20 minutes – normally it took 35 minutes. We arrived at the theatre about ten past seven and then I had a full character make-up to put on, including a wig, which usually took me a good half hour. I was the first character to appear on the stage with a 'Tea, Vicar?' sort of line, pouring out a cup of tea. *Never* have cups and saucers rattled so noisily on stage before.

Everybody enjoyed that production – except me . . . and I resolved never again!

In 1977 I visited Jersey with Pat Phoenix who was going there to open a new restaurant. I wanted to reconnoitre the island with a view to taking mother there for a holiday. Pat and I arrived at Ringway Airport and I was surprised to learn that we were going to fly from the private section. When we got to the tarmac there were two planes waiting. One was about 40 feet long, the other was *tiny*. I set out towards the larger of the two, but was deflected to the other – it held only six people, including the pilot. We were all packed in like sardines, Pat and I, two PA people and a man from Granada. I thought it would never get off the ground, but it did, and seemed to walk all the way to Jersey, taking two and a half hours to get there. 'I'll swim back,' I decided, which was brave of me, remembering my prowess in the water.

Later in the year I took mother on a regular flight, and we were enjoying ourselves when a telephone call ordered me back to Manchester. There was to be a Royal Variety Performance at the Palace Theatre in honour of the Queen's Silver Jubilee, and the cast of *Coronation Street* was bidden to provide a 15 minute sketch, written by John Stevenson. Rehearsals started as soon as I got back and proceeded rapidly.

I was chosen to be 'anchor man', on stage for the whole 15 minutes, while the others came on, said their bit and went off again. In the sketch Hilda had lost her way while trying to catch a glimpse of the Queen. The cast was nervous, naturally, but I was not expecting Violet Carson of all people to forget her lines. She nearly did, and stood there, face getting redder and arms pumping away at her sides, then at the last moment she managed to get out her line about Bonnie Prince Charlie and his soldiers marching through Manchester towards London. My reply was, 'I didn't know Prince Charles had been in the army, I thought he were in the navy . . .' At least Prince Philip laughed!

The sketch ended when I pushed Bunny off stage in a handcart covered by a Union Jack because he had drunk too much while waiting to see the Queen. 'I'm only doing what she'd be doing if her husband was exhausted,' was my exit line and it brought the house down. Pushing the handcart with Bunny in it nearly brought me down too. Afterwards at the line-up backstage we were all squashed in a narrow corridor and I was jammed against a projecting wall. As the Queen advanced in our directon I had realised from the rehearsal that when I curtseyed I would be pitched forward by the wall and would probably butt her in the stomach. So I hissed to the man next to me, 'When you've bowed, can you move to your left, please, to give me more room?' which he did, and my curtsey was a model of what a curtsey should be. I was so relieved that I immediately forgot what the Queen said to me. I returned to Jersey the next day to finish my holiday, pleased that Hilda had again upheld the honour of the Ogdens.

The next time I met the Queen was in 1982 when a new life-size set of *Coronation Street*, across Grape Street from the Television Centre, replaced the smaller-scale street built 14 years before. It was a very grand occasion. The Royal Party was escorted by Sir Denis Forman, chairman of the Granada company, and David Plowright, managing director. They met Andrew Quinn, general manager, and four veterans of the programme: Bill Podmore, the longest serving producer, Harry Kershaw, writer, producer and executive, Tony Warren, the writer who had created *The Street*, and Denis Parkin, the designer of the new lay-out.

The cast were lined up at their front doors, dressed in *Street* clothes. I had planned to appear in my curlers, but it was decided that I ought not to, so Hilda's hair was in its best frizz and she wore her Sunday best floral print. Bernard offered to clean the Palace windows, but the Queen told him it would take a very long time, there were so many of them. It was a very exciting day, bright and sunny too, for a change, and a great tribute to *The Street*'s 20 years' achievements.

Perhaps the most unlikely visitor *The Street* ever had was the late Poet Laureate, Sir John Betjeman. He was the most enthusiastic person we ever had in the studio, clapping his hands with childish delight and exclaiming, 'I can't believe I'm actually here!' Apparently he was specially fond of 'Hilda and her ghastly husband' and insisted on being photographed with them. On Mondays and Wednesdays he was in Paradise . . .

Another devoted fan of *The Street* and particularly of the Ogdens was the late Arthur Marshall. When he was due to be given the *This is Your Life* treatment Bunny and I were asked to record a little scene in character, wishing him a happy evening. We would have liked to be there in person but we were working to a tight schedule and it was not possible. Soon afterwards I received a letter from him, one that I shall always cherish:

Dear Jean Alexander,
You couldn't possibly have given me a happier This is Your Life *surprise than your marvellous appearance on March 15th. You were a dear*

creature to do it and it gave me and everybody else such pleasure. You will know how widely you are loved both for yourself and that wonderful performance and it was the high spot of the evening (and I'm not forgetting Alice Faye!). My friends in the village here, nine of whom turned up, are in ecstasies and speak of nothing else! I'm lucky enough to be a friend of Master Harty's and so one day we might just meet and I so look forward. Heartfelt thanks from a very admiring and grateful
    Arthur Marshall

CHAPTER 16

Family Interlude

1968 LOOKED like being a good year for me and the family. We had been on our third cruise and we were thinking seriously about moving house. Sefton Street was pleasant enough but we decided we would prefer a larger place. However, before we could do anything about it my father was taken ill and had to go into hospital. He was very poorly and we were extremely worried. Even though he seemed to improve quickly during his stay there I felt I had to know exactly what was wrong with him, and I determined to break through the barrier of silence that is often found among doctors. I went to see the Registrar and told him quite plainly that I had to know. So he told me: it was lung cancer and the prognosis was not good; six months was about all we could hope for.

It was a big burden having to keep the news to myself. Dad came out of hospital after a couple of weeks and maintained his improvement. He would potter about the garden, do a little gentle shopping and gave few signs of how grave his condition really was. I was on tenterhooks the whole time. Every time he sneezed or coughed I wondered – is this a signal that the end is near? But six months went by and dad continued to stay well, then a year, and I began to feel a stirring of hope; could the doctor's pessimism have been unjustified, perhaps the illness had been wrongly diagnosed. It was just before Christmas, 1969 that dad had a serious relapse. He went into hospital again, but the disease had taken too firm a grip on him and he died quite quickly and very peacefully. He was 74 years old and had worked until he was 67.

It was a big enough blow for me, who had been expecting it for so long, but for my mother it was quite shattering. They had had a long and happy married life. They had gone through hard times together and were now enjoying the comfort they deserved, and it had suddenly been cut short. But mother bore it with the fortitude one would expect from someone with her strength of character. Now we two were together and had to make fresh plans.

In the January after dad died a house which seemed to fulfil all our needs came on the market. I was anxious to move because new surroundings would help mother to get over his death and give her the incentive to cultivate new interests. So we went to view the house and liked it very much. The asking price was £6,500. This was in 1970 before house prices had started to rocket. Mother was, as I anticipated, doubtful. 'It's a lot of money, Jean,' she said. 'Don't you think we should wait a bit – prices might come down.'

'Come down!' I said. 'There's not much hope of that. The only way prices will go is up!' I was quickly proved right; the following year the house would have been worth at least £2,000 more. I made a successful offer and then we put Sefton Street on the market. We had made a lot of improvements, added a new kitchen, re-tiled the roof and turned the original wilderness into a fine garden. We sold it for £4,000. As for the new house, we both felt when we stepped over the threshold that we were going to be happy in it. I have always found that the atmosphere of a house communicates itself to me very quickly. A happy house radiates a welcome. I had felt a similar frisson of pleasure when Barbara and I first discovered Sefton Street so I was overjoyed to experience it again. The new house was situated in a wide road; it was semi-detached, with a small, neat front garden and a much larger one at the back. The inside, though larger than the one we had left, was easily manageable. All that, plus friendly neighbours, made for a very successful move.

For 12 years mother and I shared the house and the longer we were there the fonder of it we grew. We both had an obsession with tidiness and order and everything sat in its right place and *shone*. I did most of the garden myself, even the heavy work, lifting flagstones, digging up old bushes and hedges, getting dirty, with aching back and blistered hands, and I loved every minute of it. I think both house and garden expressed our personalities, and opening the front door after an absence was more than just 'coming home', it was like being enveloped in one's own skin, welcomed with loving arms and a whispered, 'So glad you're back.'

Twelve happy years, then in the spring of 1980, when mother was 84, she became troubled with circulation failure in one foot, which led to gangrene and the necessity of having a leg amputated. This was in June and immediately after the operation she was as bright as a button. I went to see her in hospital that evening; she was sitting up in bed calling for a cup of tea. It was amazing. Then she went into a Nursing home, only five minutes walk from home. She was very happy there and was looked after most sensitively. She was there until October and we were beginning to think about a return home, but just then her heart decided that it could take the strain no longer and she faded away. Fortunately I had been written out of the programme for the following week. I phoned to tell Joyce. Her first words were, 'When do you want me to come over?' and next day she was on the doorstep. I have been lucky in my friends. Needless to say, Ken and Cynthia were a tower of strength in a very difficult time.

Tears do not come easily to me and I did not cry when mother died, though the pain of her leaving seared my heart. We had been so close. She treated me as though I were still about 14, fussed over my health, my small appetite, would I be warm enough in that thin frock, you really should take an umbrella – she was the typical mum, and one could not ask for a better.

She loved the fact that I was in *Coronation Street*. Long before I ever considered the possibility of joining the cast she would say, 'You ought to get into *Coronation Street*, it would be the making of you.' And when I did become Hilda Ogden she was thrilled. 'There you are, you see,' she said, 'I told you years ago you should get in.' 'Mother, it doesn't work like that,' I tried to explain,'You have to be asked!' But I think she never quite understood the workings of agents, auditions and interviews.

She never boasted to anybody that I was the famous Hilda Ogden; in fact, she was rather cagey about it, not wanting people to make her acquaintance in order to approach me. She tended to remain in the background at any function we attended, relishing the attention that I received, but never pushing herself forward. No stage mother, she.

She enjoyed the cruises we went on right into the 1970s. In 1971 we went on the *Andes* to the West Indies. To see her standing on the edge of the water on the beach at Barbados was a great joy. She had never been as near to the sea even when we used to go to Rhyl. 'Go on, mum, stand *in* the water and I'll take your photograph,' I said.

'I'm not going in there,' she said firmly.

'But it's only three inches deep. What harm can it do you?'

So she tentatively advanced a few inches, till the water just covered her feet. I was getting the camera ready when a little wave, two inches high, crawled round her ankles. 'Jean!' she screamed. 'Come and get me – the tide's coming in!'

Just before Christmas, 1981 Joyce invited me to York to spend a few days in my favourite city. I was in light-hearted mood as I caught the train on Saturday morning; no commitments until the following Tuesday . . .

On Monday morning there was a telephone call for me. It was my next door neighbour telling me that my house was flooded. 'You'd better come back immediately!' he said.

When I got home Eric Sloman was waiting for me. 'I'll take you in to have a look at the damage,' he said, 'then you must come and stay with us for as long as is necessary.' He took a torch and we went in. The first thing I was aware of was water squelching over my shoes as I walked over the hall carpet. Eric shone his torch around, and when I saw the extent of the damage I should have felt black despair. But for some reason I laughed instead, not hysterically, just disbelievingly. The devastation was so over the top – like a bit of ham acting in the theatre. 'You've gone too far this time!' I wanted to say.

Eric had found a plumber who had stopped the flooding, and he and his wife Monica had done their best to clean up a bit, but nothing could disguise the fact that more than half the house was impossible to live in, and that major repairs and redecoration would be necessary. The initial drying out presented quite a problem because I could not get a flow of air through the house; all the windows and back doors had been closed and the water had caused them to swell so much that they couldn't be opened. Only the front door was functioning properly.

By a lucky chance the front room and my bedroom, which was above it, had escaped, but the back of the house was saturated. Wallpaper had fallen off in great sheets, leaving dark-stained plaster in place of the original pink. Upstairs, beds and carpets were completely ruined, while below, the veneer of my mahogany dining-table rose up like a mountain in the centre and had split right across. In the kitchen the cupboards and the cooker were waterlogged. The whole place looked as though it had been thoroughly vandalised by Mother Nature; in fact, the cause of the trouble was traced to the feed to the main water tank in the loft, which had cracked, then split and allowed the water to pour out.

For the next few months life was an extended camping out. I was able to get an electrician to fix a temporary connection from the meter to the central heating boiler – and I had it on, full blast, day and night until the walls had finally dried out so the re-wiring could be completed. I had to live by candle-light; romantic, but not very practical. I was working at the studio during the day, so could temporarily forget the horrors of my dear little semi, but when I returned home in the evening I found the house full of steam from the action of the central heating, and had to leave the front door open to allow the steam to escape.

Slowly things began to improve. The house gradually dried out. New windows had to be put in, and doors shaved and re-hung. The decorators arrived, stripped things down to the bare wood or plaster and began replacing from scratch the decorations I had been so fond of. I bought new carpets, new beds, a new dining-table, and at the end of the second week in May the house was back to normal and the flood might never have happened. My traumatic experience had lasted for five months, its horror only lessened by the goodwill of my neighbours and by my own fortitude; rarely have I been so pleased with myself for not giving in to despair, but it's the sort of situation I never want to face again . . .

CHAPTER 17

Making the Decision

WHEN Bernard Youens died in 1984 it was a shattering blow to everybody in *Coronation Street*. We all admired this gentle and cultured man whose talent had created a truly great character in Stan Ogden.

Bernard had not had an easy life before he came into *The Street* but he was a hard worker and had the enormous blessing of a happy marriage to his wife Edna, known as Teddy. I have said earlier how he and I hit it off both personally and professionally from our very first meeting, yet we rarely met outside the studio. We did do some personal appearances for various charities in the sixties. Teddy and he came over to Southport a couple of times and prior to a PA I would go to their house before going off in Bunny's car. I did not drive so it was always his car. The Press frequently tried to place some sinister significance in the two of us going off together. On the 'no smoke without fire' principle they were always throwing out hints and ferreting around for a juicy bit of scandal. But if they wanted the story of a marriage breaking up they were wasting their time. There was absolutely nothing but personal appearances that took Bunny and me out together. This was one occasion where there was not only no smoke without fire, but no smoke!

Bunny's health suffered considerably after his first heart attack but he was never a man to give in and he fought gamely against the after-effects. Even after a stroke which left him with impaired speech he countered by having speech therapy, and went most of the way to conquering the impediment. But the dice were loaded too heavily against him and he had a further stroke. Due to a past history of arthritis he began to have difficulty in lifting his head properly; but still he battled on, motivated, I think, by his own pride and determination to recover from the illnesses and by his devotion to Teddy and his family. He worked until the very last minute, but finally he had to go into hospital. As a last cruel blow a leg had to be amputated. Soon after that he died.

Though Bernard Youens had died Stanley Ogden was presumed to be still alive. When, after a decent interval, Stan died in the storyline, the writers treated it with great tact and sensitivity, and I would like to think that my own performance as the bereaved Hilda was as sensitive. I think it was recognised as such as it was that particular performance, I gather, for which I was honoured with the Royal Television Society Best Performance Award. Yet I have to stress that it was only a performance. I did not bring any of my real sorrow to the screen. After all, Bunny had died some months earlier. I could not have allowed my real feelings to intrude in the scene as it would have meant I had lost control of the situation, and that would have been wrong. To have let go would have been unfair to me and to the memory of Bunny.

Script, direction, lighting and my own technique were the reasons the scene was so poignant. It seemed to affect many millions of viewers. For me, it was acting – I was giving a performance.

1987 was the year when I made the most momentous decision of my life – to leave *The Street*. There was no single reason for the decision, nor was there a single identifiable moment when I made it. Reasons crept up on me gradually. Bernard's death, for instance, affected me deeply and later, when it was reflected in the programme as Stan's death, it became clear that the end of the partnership meant significant changes to Hilda's position in future stories.

For a while the writers showed interest in the character, bringing Kevin Webster to lodge at No. 13, and later Sally Seddon as his wife, and there was the introduction of Uncle Tom, Sally's green-grocer uncle. Uncle Tom was a dead end though, as I had no intention of countenancing any sort of serious romance. The Hilda I had created and knew so well would never re-marry. So Uncle Tom had to go. But that meant my story lines grew thinner, and I seemed peripheral to the various plots. Yes, it was getting nearer to the time to go.

Another factor was my age. I had been in *Coronation Street* for 23 years and I had had my 60th birthday. Sixty is not old nowadays, and I certainly did not feel my age, but I desperately wanted to do other things, play different parts, spread my wings, as it were, in the years ahead, the same feeling I had had all those years ago when I decided to leave Southport and York. No more theatre but, I hoped, more television, with opportunities to show my versatility.

A third motive for leaving was rather more prosaic: I was so tired with the travel that was involved with the job. The daily round of waiting for trains and knowing that I would have an uncomfortable journey was taking its toll. So much time seemed to be spent in trains between Manchester and Southport, with bitterly cold waits in Salford Station. The Southport line appeared to be something of a Cinderella line and trains were always breaking down. I have waited over an hour for a train after a breakdown only to find that the replacement had broken down too. When eventually one got away, the two carriages would be filled to capacity, the poor passengers almost hanging on to the sides. Many a time I have travelled as far as Wigan in the luggage van, with 40 or so other people, and the old diesels were either freezing cold in winter or furnace-like in summer. After a third of a lifetime putting up with such treatment I could think of better ways of occupying my time.

I read a rather odd comment in a newspaper suggesting that Granada should have sent a car to fetch me from Southport every morning and taken me back home at night. I certainly did not expect it and they never considered it. I chose to live in Southport. Tedious though the journey was, I much preferred sleeping in my own bed to staying at a hotel in Manchester all week, even though I would have received overnight stay money.

The usual pattern was quite straightforward. I had a taxi from home to take me to the station at Southport. At first the journey to Manchester took about 55 minutes but, as British Rail got more efficient, it took an hour and twenty minutes! Salford Station was only five minutes walk from Granada, fortunately. After the day's work I reversed the process; train to Southport and taxi home. I came to know many of the taxi drivers very well, and found them all friendly and helpful. If I missed the Salford train I had to walk to Victoria Station to catch a much later and slower train which did not get me home until after nine o'clock, and in the dark winter months it was not pleasant. Even so, that was preferable to sitting in a hotel room and twiddling my thumbs. If Granada had provided me with a car it would have cost them about £30 a day, and I was not a big enough star to warrant that expense!

A friend once told me that I was lucky to have the train journey as it was an ideal opportunity to learn my lines. Not so – I never took my script home with me. I did my learning in the firm's time, something I could do with ease after my years of learning a massive role nearly every week. The only exception to this routine was when we were filming on a Monday morning without a rehearsal for the scene. I had to know the lines from the outset. Then I would just take the relevant scene home with me and have it ready for Monday morning. Otherwise I would arrive at the studio for rehearsal, sit down with a cup of tea and learn my first scene, and the automatic timer in my head could cope with any scene long or short. So during the day I would keep one scene ahead, learning my next scene while those I were not in were being rehearsed. It did not take me long to have both episodes fixed firmly in my memory, and when the day's work was over I felt completely free. I walked out of the studio as Jean Alexander, not Hilda Ogden. Finally, I was beginning to find the weekly routine in getting the programmes out increasingly irksome. I had been a slave to routine all my working life, and I wanted to be free.

Preparing two half hour programmes was very different from the rehearsing and playing that weekly Rep demanded, but the concentration that was needed was equally fierce, and the mechanics of recording meant a high standard of technical accomplishment. Though most evenings might be free the hours spent in the rehearsal room and in the studio amounted to more than those spent rehearsing on stage.

Monday morning was reserved for outside filming, either in the street or further afield on location. This had to be done speedily and efficiently (the process occasionally delayed by inappropriate weather), because rehearsals for the new episodes started at 2 p.m. These were in the nature of improvisations; we had no sets or furniture and only rudimentary or imaginary props. The outline of the set walls was marked by tape so that we should not stray through the scenery. The director with his camera script, which contained as many as 200 shots distributed among up to four cameras, plotted each scene methodically, working out exits, entrances and standing or moving positions. All these we had to remember with great accuracy. A wrong move, a position too far forward, one step too far to the left or right could mask another character, kill a line or make the cameraman's work more difficult. Before the end of the day we had made known our requirements for the clothes we would need. Mine were usually simple; curlers, pinny and head scarf, and the famous mac that lasted so long it almost fell off me when I put it on.

Rehearsals continued on Tuesday. Now we could devote much more attention to the script, to interpreting our parts; we could ask the director for advice and sometimes, perhaps, question a piece of dialogue, even a single word, as not being in character. I occasionally had to cut one of Hilda's malapropisms. I was insistent that they should sound 'real' – the sort of thing that Hilda would really get confused over; those which were put in for the sake of an easy laugh or were inconsistent with her level of intelligence were out.

Wednesday mornings – more rehearsals until lunchtime. In the afternoon came a technical run in which the lighting director was involved, also the technical supervisor, the senior cameraman, the sound supervisor, and the producer, who was responsible for the overall artistic interpretation. Camera, sound and lighting problems, if any, were sorted out. Even the writers had their say, bemoaning the disappearance of favourite lines, or substituting words and phrases that suddenly did not sound right. At the end of Wednesday the episodes were slowly taking shape, still not perfect, but good enough to draw a sigh of satisfaction from the harassed director.

When the cast had gone their several ways on Wednesday evenings the sets were built and furnished. The Ogden home received its 'muriel' and Stan's armchair, the *Rovers Return* its bar, and the factory its sewing machines and bales of material. On Thursday morning the studio was given over to the electricians and the lighting director. At

1 p.m. the scenic designer took over and a horde of props men dressed the sets, right down to the last ashtray on the bar, the crucifix on Ivy Tilsley's wall, the frying pans in the café, the newspapers on the *Kabin* counter and the flying ducks on the Ogden's wall (the middle one always askew – I checked that personally!). Then the last rehearsals took place, each scene repeated until both the director and cast were satisfied. Cameras and sound equipment were at the ready and then the scenes were recorded on video-tape. What complicated matters was the fact that the scenes were not shot in sequence, but rather as the director determined – those taking place in the pub, for instance, followed one another even though one might take place at the beginning and the other at the end of the programme. It seemed bitty at the time and demanded some mental readjustment, but the method was accepted as being more efficient and less time-wasting.

Friday was the final workday for that week. The schedule was similar to Thursdays, except that we worked from 9.30 a.m. to 6.30 in the evening, our longest working day. We were immensely relieved at the end of Friday at the prospect of two full days off, though the spectre of Monday was never far away. But we were lucky; the director and his team had to spend their weekend editing all the tapes for next week's transmission.

When we were not wanted on set for rehearsal or recording we had a Green Room with comfortable chairs, personal cubicles partitioned off, where we could learn lines, answer fan mail or just chat with friends.

When I had finally thought things through and made my decision it was getting near the time for my contract to be re-negotiated, a job that I always left to Joan Reddin. With my courage screwed to the sticking-point I walked into Bill Podmore's office. I saw by the look on his face that he knew why I was there, so there was no need to beat about the bush. 'Bill, I've decided to go,' I said simply, and waited for his reaction.

He gave me a rueful but friendly smile. 'I've been expecting you to say that for a long time,' he said. 'And you haven't made the decision lightly, have you?'

'I've been thinking about it for about a year,' I admitted.

'I guessed that,' he said, 'and I know you want to try other things. I suppose I can't persuade you ... no, I see I can't.'

I nodded. He got up and came round his desk to shake my hand. 'Good luck, Jean. We shall miss you,' he said, and I knew he meant it.

And that was all. No dramatics, tears or recriminations. A report in one of the tabloids that he would allow me to write my own new contract and determine my own salary if only I would stay was absolute nonsense. Neither of us would insult the other by suggesting such an over-the-top ploy. I left *Coronation Street* with the friendliest of feelings on both sides and that is the way it always will be.

I was not so naive as to think that I could slide out of *The Street* without publicity from the Press, but I was not prepared for either the hyperbole of the tabloid feature writers or for the scale of the praise and affection shown by my colleagues in the programme. I felt very flattered and very humble. On the whole the Press comments were predictable. Myths were perpetuated and inaccuracies repeated – but who was I to complain? At least I had not been attacked with the venom that some people in the cast had, with a mixture of truth, half truth and lies that are impossible to fight against. I was gratified by the headlines that expressed affectionate regard for the character: 'CHEERIO CHUCK!' from *The Star*; 'TA-RA CHUCK!' from *The News of the World*; 'CHEERS CHUCK' from *Weekend*; and I was awfully tempted to reply 'CHUCK IT, CHUCKS!'

I was besieged by journalists from all over the country, all of whom wanted desperately to have an exclusive interview concerning my departure. (When I said 'No' some of them just made one up!) As I have a number of friends in the profession I should have been in a dilemma over someone to write 'the big one'. But I was not. There was only one person I wanted to do it, the person to whom I, and so many other actors in *The Street*, owe so much, the creator of the whole thing, Tony Warren. I had known and liked him for years and I knew that he would be accurate, sympathetic and truthful. So it was Tony Warren's articles that appeared in *The People* in 1987, and they were as good and well-written as I had anticipated.

Among the tributes I received I got a special joy from reading Donald Bodley's comments in the *Yorkshire Free Press*. As one would expect there was no highfaluting nonsense. 'She was a very good actress and obviously cut out for character roles ... a quiet, studious girl with a nice sense of humour . . . we have been delighted to see her become a national figure on TV.'

And now I have to put modesty aside and write about some of the things my colleagues have said, not in a spirit of conceit but to express my thanks to them for all their generosity. To Bill Roache, for instance, for his warm comments on the memorable and, for me, traumatic *Arsenic and Old Lace* at Oldham, as well as on my Hilda performances. I loved Brian Mosley's account of the York pantomime in which we both appeared thirty years ago and I hope I can supply 'plenty of surprises in the future', as he suggested.

Betty Driver wrote that she is 'proudest of all that Jean and I are best friends', and I reciprocate that feeling. I shall miss her every bit as much as she will me. We had met on the set more than 17 years before; we began talking then and have not stopped talking since. Lynne Perrie and Bill Waddington, among many others, said nice things about me, but I must admit to a special feeling of pride in some of the youngsters' comments. These lively young people were a tonic to us older ones, their energy and enthusiasm even making us a bit envious. I was particularly touched by Michael Le Vell, who said that whenever he received his scripts for the following week he had a quick look through to see if he had a scene with 'Mrs O' because he knew that would be the best one; and by Sally Whittaker, who said that I was always keen to make her feel at ease and how in future whatever she might be playing she would wonder 'how would Jean play this . . .' It was one of my great pleasures to see how well Michael and Sally grew into their parts.

After the recording of the last episode I was in at Christmas 1987, I was invited to dinner in the Penthouse at Granada with David Plowright, Harry Kershaw, Bill Podmore, and some of the writers and their wives. It was a wonderful evening in an atmosphere that was a sort of distillation of the goodness and generosity of the Granada management. They gave me a superb Lalique model of a crouching cat. Nothing in the world could have pleased me more and I wondered how they knew that I longed to have this particular piece. Apparently Bill Podmore had asked Betty Driver if she could suggest something I would really like. Betty remembered how I had raved to her about a Lalique cat that I had seen while on holiday but had found it too heavy to carry back. Bill had found out where to get it and duly bought it for me. But that was not all . . . They had another surprise which was equally welcome. David Plowright, who is Lord Olivier's brother-in-law, aware of my great admiration for the actor, had asked him to inscribe one of the stills from the magnificent *King Lear* which Olivier had done for Granada a few years before. It was presented to me beautifully framed and today has pride of place on my staircase wall.

As for my friends in the cast of *Coronation Street* – their generosity was overwhelming. They knew that my favourite composer is Beethoven (not Mozart, as one paper claimed) and they gave me tapes of all the symphonies by Karajan and the Berlin Philharmonic Orchestra, the piano concertos played by Vladimir Ashkenazy and the complete piano sonatas played by Alfred Brendel. A cornucopia of superb music that I derive great joy from hearing. I was reminded of the £14 record player I bought in London when I received my first *Television Club* cheque. I could only afford one record, Beethoven's Seventh Symphony, which I played over and over again until it was worn out. Also from the cast there was a gilt medallion in a box from a Manchester jeweller, a token to the value of £100 which I can spend at any time. I still have it – I want to wait until I can find the perfect memento.

Writing about these gifts reminds me, poignantly, of another occasion some years ago. When Hilda and Stan went to visit their son Trevor in his posh home in Derbyshire there was, on the studio set, a lovely china owl of pale blue and white, with eyes like pansies. It was an exquisite thing and I admired it so much I asked the prop man where I could buy one. He told me that all the set decorations were hired, but he would do his best to get one for me. 'I'll buy it,' I said, 'and I'll pay you now, if you wish.' But he said he had better first find out if it were available. A few weeks later a parcel arrived for me in the Green Room. It was the owl! I hurried down to the properties department during my lunch break and found the prop buyer. 'Thank you so much,' I said, 'how much do I owe you?' He smiled. 'You don't – Bunny bought it.' It turned out that Bunny had heard me asking about it, had a quiet word with the prop man and bought it for my birthday. It was a typically kind and thoughtful gesture. The china owl and the Lalique cat now sit in silent but friendly communication in my sitting-room.

CHAPTER 18

'It is You, Isn't it?'

IN MAY, 1986, Bee's, the Chester firm of seedsmen, wrote to tell me that they had a new rose they were about to launch and they would like to call it after me. There was already a rose called 'Alexander', so would I agree to 'Our Hilda'? I gave my permission enthusiastically. I could not imagine anything more delightful than to be associated with a rose!

'Our Hilda' appeared in her raspberry pink glory at the Chelsea Flower Show that year and I was invited down to the preview. I had never been to the show before and I was entranced by the variety and beauty of the exhibits, but for me 'Our Hilda' shone the brightest. With the 'Betty Driver' rose it now takes pride of place in my garden. 'Betty Driver' is pale pink and we make a lovely couple (of roses!).

I stayed in London for a couple of days and contacted Joan Reddin, whom I had not seen for some time. To celebrate our reunion we decided to have dinner at the Ritz. Just as we had been given the menus the pianist, at a white grand piano, began to play the *Coronation Street* theme tune very quietly. Joan's eyes nearly popped out. 'Well,' she said, 'I've never seen anything like this before. You come down to London once in five years and the whole town's jumping! A rose named after you and recognition at the Ritz!'

'A slight exaggeration,' I said, but I really was astonished. It was not the sort of thing one would expect at the Ritz. I made a little face at the pianist and wiggled my fingers, and he bowed slightly and went on playing. 'Joan,' I said, 'in the days when I lived in London and I used to walk to the Labour Exchange twice a week I used to pass the Ritz and I often wondered what it would be like to go inside. But I could not have afforded even a cup of tea, and my shoes needed mending.'

'Yes,' Joan agreed drily, 'funny how things work out, isn't it?'

Then a man and his wife who had been dining at the next table got up and came over to us. 'We would just like to tell you how much we enjoy *Coronation Street*,' one of them murmured.

'So pleased,' I replied. I inclined my head graciously and wondered what grandpa Hill would have said . . .

May 23, 1985 saw my career crowned with an unexpected accolade that I would not in my wildest dreams have thought possible. I won the Royal Television Society's Award for Best Performance for 1984/85. It was presented by Sir Huw Wheldon, the President of the Society, at the Annual Ball at Grosvenor House, and was a truly glittering occasion. I wore a new black dress and thought I looked quite elegant.

'She has delighted literally hundreds of millions of viewers with the comedy and pathos she has brought to her starring role in Britain's top soap opera,' Sir Huw said. To say that I felt honoured to follow in the footsteps of Timothy West, Celia Johnson, Sir Michael Horden, Alan Bates and Dame Peggy Ashcroft is an understatement . . . I was equally delighted by the fact that at last the seal of respectability had been given to TV soap operas by the award. But all I could think of to say when I accepted it was, 'Half this award is for Bernard Youens, because I could not have done it without him. I'm sure he would be glad and I'm only sorry he isn't here to see it. If he had been I'm sure it would have been a double award' – words which really came from my heart.

I had not told any member of the cast about my trip to London because the whole thing was supposed to be very hush-hush. Granada gave me the day off and I was escorted to London by David Plowright and other officials, and Granada paid for all my expenses. Granada is a very generous company and looks after its people in a very caring way.

Two years later another honour came my way. A readers' poll for *TV Times* voted me Best TV Actress of 1986. The award ceremony took place at Thames's Teddington Studio and the award was presented to me by Russell Harty. I felt very flattered that so many viewers liked my 'Hilda'.

The BLHO (British League for Hilda Ogden) was formed at an

extraordinary general meeting in 1979, so secretly that one or two of the original members did not even know that it had taken place. It so happened that it was the first and only meeting of the League . . .

The Founding Five were: Laurence Olivier, President; Willis Hall, Treasurer; Sir John Betjeman, Chairman; Michael Parkinson, Recruiting Officer; and Russell Harty, Secretary. They felt that Hilda Ogden, 'a national monument', deserved proper recognition for the service she had given to the nation, principally in having to put up with Stan, the 'muriel' and the ducks. I graciously agreed to the foundation of the League, but I must say that Michael Parkinson made a fine mess of his job, doing nothing whatsoever to drum up recruits for the worthy cause. Five thousand tin badges were printed bearing a picture of Hilda in heated Carmen rollers, and they were worn at the inaugural tea party at the Garrick Club. He managed to get rid of two of these priceless insignia, to whom it's not known. Not good enough, Michael! Sadly Sir John Betjeman and Russell Harty have left us and I think the BLHO has gone into liquidation. But it was fun while it lasted.

Other honours have been heaped upon me. I was once a mascot for a year for a Welsh Rugby Club, each member of which had to produce a curler at every meeting, otherwise he would be fined; and I was made an honorary member of the Seamen's Union after a spell of filming on a little Spanish ship in Bootle Dock on a wet Monday morning. It was supposed to be a cruise ship sailing to the Caribbean . . .

Letters – they have been both a blessing and a curse ever since Hilda started to become popular. The majority of them were simple fan letters, and no actress minds getting them; when they don't come is the time for worrying. Answering letters has always been something of a chore for me – my friends know that only too well – but I just had to discipline myself and sit down and answer the stacks that piled up on my dressing-table. Some of the letters I received went far beyond the reasonable and I am still amazed at the brazen cheek of some of my correspondents. One woman, having read somewhere that I enjoyed cruises, wrote to say that she too would very much like to go on one and thought it would be nice to go with me. She only had enough money for incidental expenses. Would I, therefore, buy her ticket and let her know when and where she should meet me to join the ship?

Another woman wrote peremptorily to ask me to send her £16,000 immediately as she wished to start a play school in her town and she had found the ideal property for that price. Would I be quick though as the house would not be available for much longer. I did not reply but she was a very determined lady for after a month or so I got an even more forthright letter telling me to send the money *at once*. The first house, she explained, had been sold to someone else, but another had just come on the market, even more suitable. 'Please send the money by return!' She must have thought I was very mean and discourteous when she still got no reply.

Two letters which I found rather charming came from old ladies in their eighties, from different parts of the country and quite independently. The gist of them was that they had known me slightly when they were on the stage as dancers and had worked with me when I was a soubrette with Shaun Glenville and Dorothy Ward! One of them sent me a photograph. Sure enough, it was of Jean Alexander, signed with a great flourish, but a Jean Alexander of demure and coy appearance; it must have been taken long before I was born. I wrote to both of them explaining that they had made a mistake, but I wonder if they still think I am the Jean Alexander of their youth.

There were a great number of letters from people who believed that Hilda Ogden was a real person, even to the extent of sending her money to buy something without letting Stan know. (Bernard received similar letters, telling him not to let Hilda know). Of course I returned the money when they gave a return address, otherwise the Angioscope Fund was a pound or two richer. I was offered cleaning and housekeeping jobs, holidays away from Stan, new pinnys and curlers – if I had indeed been Hilda I would have had a much easier life. Occasionally there was a letter of rebuke, like the one that suggested that I would never make any kind of headway in the theatre unless I learned to speak properly and got rid of my dreadful Northern accent! I particularly enjoyed getting letters from children and have a feeling that they saw Hilda as a jolly and understanding mum who would be fun to have around the house. As one little boy of six wrote: 'I would like you as my mum because you would be strict but you would let me have chips.'

*

Being recognised in the street when going about one's daily business can be quite dangerous at times. I was once in Marks & Spencer's Food Department when a push from behind sent me head first into the Vegetable Lasagne and Spaghetti Bolognaise. I struggled upright, wondering whether there was an earthquake in progress, only to find myself face to face with a red-faced woman, grinning from ear to ear. 'There you are, Fern,' she said to the small child clinging to her skirt, 'I told you, didn't I? It is you, isn't it?' she added, shoving her face close to mine.

'Yes, I am me,' I said, politely but weakly. That seemed to satisfy her. She walked away, chatting excitedly to Fern. My back was sore for days.

Not long afterwards I was coming out of Woolworth's when a figure bore down on me and shoved me hard up against the window. For a moment I thought I was being mugged in broad daylight and I clutched my handbag tightly. But no, my assailant, another large woman, pointed a finger at me. 'I know who you are,' she said. Then she backed away, staring at me as though I were a priceless painting in the National Gallery, suddenly turned and went off. It is difficult to know what to say in those circumstances.

It would be foolish to mind being recognised but I do find people's reactions somewhat odd. Sometimes a person will say, 'You are Jean Alexander, aren't you? May I have your autograph?' Then, however minute or grubby the scrap of paper thrust under my nose, I am pleased to sign it. The same applies when I am identified as Hilda Ogden, though I am tired of, 'Where's your curlers?' or, 'Where's Stan, then?' It is the other gambits that make me want to giggle: 'It is, isn't it?' or, 'Are you who I think you are?' or, 'I've *seen* you!'

One of the oddest encounters happened soon after I had left *The Street* and was visiting friends in a small country town. After dining in the local inn we were having a drink in the lounge. Several people, including the manager and the chef, had already asked for my autograph. As we were chatting a middle-aged woman approached and went through the 'I've seen you on the telly' routine. I smiled and agreed that she had indeed seen me, and she went on to say how much she enjoyed the programme and my part in it. As she bent over I realised she was very slowly sinking to her knees, and in a moment she was on the floor in front of me, still talking. I felt terrible – nobody had ever knelt to me before and I wondered for a mad moment whether she was expecting the laying on of hands. By this time conversation had dried up completely. She stayed where she was, smiling somewhat foolishly, then it struck me that she *couldn't* get up, that her rheumatism had got the better of her. So my friends and I gently helped her up. With 'I have enjoyed meeting you' she hobbled back to her own party.

One aspect of TV fame that can be very unpleasant is the constant, unrelenting attention of the Press. Unless you are very strong or determined you can be hounded, followed, spied on so that your life is not your own and you end up on the verge of paranoia. Everything you say is twisted, your words are manipulated against you, questions are so loaded that a simple answer is made to seem an admission of guilt. The lives of some of my friends in *The Street* were sometimes made unbearable by such incredibly vicious behaviour. Fortunately, I have never had anything very important to hide, but I was determined not to be harassed or pressurised, and that any interview I gave should be on my own terms. Not that it stopped reporters from trying to discover my ghastly secrets and subject me to the same unscrupulous attention as my friends. One Sunday newspaper just missed the scoop of the century: 'HILDA OGDEN'S SECRET LOVER! . . .'

My Uncle Walter and I were working in my front garden when a car drew up outside the house and two men got out. They came up to the gate. 'Miss Alexander, can we have a word with you?' one of them said.

'Who are you?' I asked.

He mentioned the name of his newspaper.

'Sorry, no,' I said.

'Oh, but we'd just like to – '

'I daresay you would,' I said, mentally brandishing the spade I held in my hand, 'but you're not getting a word out of me,' and I whisked my uncle back into the house. The men gave me disgruntled looks but returned to their car.

The following day I had to go into Southport and my uncle came with me to explore the town while I went to the hairdresser's. When we met later for lunch he said, 'I met one of those reporters on Lord Street.'

'Oh, yes,' I said, 'and what did he want?'

'Well, he came up and said he believed that I was staying with Miss Alexander. I said that I was, and then he asked me if I was your friend. He said that with a kind of leer. I told him that, yes, he could say that. Then he seemed to get very excited and asked me how long I have known you. We've been close for many years, I said. Then he almost started to drool. "What!" he yelped. Yes, I'm her uncle, I said . . .'

That seemed to end the matter. I should add that Uncle Walter was 77 years old at the time.

At one time the clamour for interviews grew so insistent that I thought I would give one or two but I would turn the situation to my advantage. So when I was approached by the *News of the World* I told their reporter that he could have an interview if I was paid for it.

'No problem,' he said. '£50 be all right?'

'£1,200,' I said.

'Hey, steady on, I don't think my editor will wear that!'

'Telephone him and ask him,' I said. 'That's my figure, take it or leave it!'

Well, the editor did agree, thinking, no doubt, that I was going to come out with something spicy. I gave the interview, revealing nothing that I had not said in any other interview, and when it was over I told the disappointed reporter to make the cheque out to the Angioscope Fund, Queen Elizabeth Hospital, Birmingham.

I made the same conditions for another interview for the *Daily Mirror*. This time the cheque was for £500. So the hospital did quite well from the tabloids!

The only interviews I have given gladly and unconditionally were to Russell Harty, Tony Warren and Jean Rook. In each case I knew the result would be well-written, witty and honest.

CHAPTER 19

Me – and Hilda

PEOPLE have often said to me, 'Is there anything of you in Hilda, or Hilda in you?' and it is not an easy question to answer. I suppose every part one plays contains some elements of one's own personality, even if you are disguised heavily as a drunken barge woman or prettified up to play a pantomime fairy; so Hilda could not help but have some part of me in her character, expressions and mannerisms. As far as I was concerned I knew Hilda well, long before I became the character.

Over the years I had picked up many bits and pieces by observing odd quirks of behaviour and storing them up in my mind for future use. When I lived in Liverpool during the war I saw girls in the tram going to work in the munition factories, all of them with curlers sticking out of their headscarves. The latter were compulsory, hair had to be covered because of dangerous machinery. As soon as they had finished work in the evening off would come the curlers and turbans, lipstick and powder would be applied, and out dancing they would go.

In Hilda Ogden's dossier, supplied when I joined the cast, she had worked on munitions during the war, so I knew exactly how she would look. Thus came the familiar Hilda that the nation took to its heart.

Bits of me in Hilda? Although I tend to be reserved and will rarely make a fuss or raise my voice in public unless something really arouses me, such as an animal being cruelly treated, and I cannot see myself having a blazing row with a neighbour (certainly not with *my* neighbours!), yet there are times when I wish I could get rid of that particular inhibition, and in Hilda I was able to do so.

I have always been a fighter too, like Hilda, in a quieter sort of way, against the blows of Fate, against depression caused by poverty, lack of work or ill-health. We have that quality in common. Hilda was also a very puritanical little creature – she disapproved of 'living over the brush', and she would not have any hanky-panky going on in her parlour, but she loved scandal, both hearing it and spreading it. Her eyes gleamed, her mouth tightened and off she scuttled to spread the bad news. She loved to be the first to broadcast Elsie Tanner's goings-on or what she had overheard in the pub, and to embroider such tittle-tattle was as natural as breathing.

We are complete opposites in that direction. Either I don't hear gossip or if I do I have forgotten it in a couple of minutes. In fact, my interest is so small that my fellow actors stopped telling me any titbits that were going the rounds. 'You remember when so-and-so did such-and-such?' Betty Driver might say.

'No,' I would reply vaguely. 'Did she?'

'But I told you only last week!' was Betty's exasperated reply. It could have been a week, a day, a year as far as I was concerned. It is amazing how many bits of news that would have had Hilda quivering with curiosity got past me.

Another way in which she and I were poles apart was where tidiness was concerned. I can't bear things cluttering up the place and I certainly do not have any flying ducks or a 'muriel'. I don't like my hair being untidy or dishes left unwashed or weeds in the garden. I can't bear noise and clatter. I might possibly have put up with Hilda as a next door neighbour because she would have been good-hearted, but I would not have wanted her popping round to borrow a cup of sugar every five minutes. I know she would have been willing to look after things when I was away, but I'm sure she would have read my private letters. On second thoughts, no! Hilda can stay in Weatherfield and I'll stick to Southport! But, bless her, she's been good to me, and there's a lot about her I admire.

My singing voice is nothing to write home about, and I have always been unwilling to sing in public because of what Ken used to say when we were children, but Hilda's efforts were even worse. The origin of that pinched nasal sound comes from my memories of being in a train going from Southport to Birkdale when I was in Rep. It was late on Saturday night and there was a party of Liverpool boys and girls on the train, all singing, 'When April show-ers . . .' in quavering, high-pitched voices; and a lot of women used to sing like that when the pubs were turning out; so when Hilda was pegging out the washing and the script said 'Sing' I came out with what I'd heard all those years ago in my chucking-out voice. Everybody fell about, thinking I was trying to be funny, but to me it was just part of the character. So the writers would occasionally put 'Hilda sings' in the script and I would oblige again, but I did not like to do it too often.

Hilda's malapropisms were also my idea and came from my own background. For instance, 'Admiralty' was always 'Admirality' in Toxteth. Again, I did not want to spoil the joke by over-doing it, so they were only inserted infrequently.

I have highlighted the differences between Hilda and me, but I have not yet assessed my own character. So I will try to sum up Jean Alexander who, from the little girl growing up in a run down corner of a large city, through her uncomplicated adolescence, first and unhappy experience of the working world, gradual absorption into the profession she had set her heart on, had, by luck and hard work, achieved the status of household name, watched by millions of people, written about, gossiped about, voted the fourth most popular woman in the country (the other three being Royals!). What has success done to her? How different is she from the struggling actress in weekly Rep? The answers are 'Nothing!' and 'No different!' I can honestly say that success and money have not altered me in the slightest. Yes, I have a mink coat, and I go on cruises and take a taxi whenever I want to, but I am truly most happy grubbing about in the garden, reading, listening to my beloved Beethoven, walking in the Lake District and enjoying the company of my friends. And my sense of humour is as ribald as ever.

I have always wanted to work for my living and shall continue to do so, even though I could play the lady of leisure for the rest of my life. Hitherto I have been a slave to routine, but now I am my own boss and that is wonderful. I do not want to be beholden to anyone and I am quite prepared to look after myself. I'm quite happy with my own company most of the time. I can't stand clutter. I think I am the tidiest person I have ever known! It may be a sign of an untidy mind but there's nothing I can do about it now . . .

I suppose I am slightly puritanical (not that I do not enjoy jokes that would have made my mother blush): that is, I have a moral basis to my thinking and actions and I try to live by the accepted tenets of Christianity; but I never preach and I never judge. I am tolerant of people whose beliefs I do not share and if they want an orgy every Tuesday night good luck to them, as long as they don't expect me to join in! Although strong-minded in many directions I am often diffident and shy, and don't like to stand out in a crowd. In fact, I am a curious jumble, as most people are, and I do not claim any outstanding virtues or vices. I'm content to be me, and my friends seem to like it that way.

A lot of nonsense has appeared in the Press at various times commenting on the fact that I have never married. Either my heart has been broken (by whom I am never quite sure), or I have broken off countless engagements, or I am still looking for Mr Right, and so on. The simple truth is: I wanted to be an actress from a very early age and I dedicated myself to achieving that ambition. Marriage was never part of that long term plan.

I know a lot of people in the theatre run marriage and a career at the same time, often very successfully, but I could never see myself having the mental or physical stamina to do that. I cannot bear doing half a job. Even before I became a professional I made a decision to be footloose, free to go where the work took me. In the dim and distant past there were boyfriends, but when I made it clear that my guiding star was to be the theatre and not the nursery we always agreed amicably to go our separate ways. After all, there are millions of women in the country who have preferred a career to marriage. I am just one of them, it's as simple as that.

My decision was helped, I suppose, by the fact that I do not have a strong maternal instinct, and I am not all that keen on babies and young children. They're all right in small quantities and if they belong to someone else; but bottle-filling, nappy-changing, sleepless nights and pram-pushing are not my idea of heaven. I might have missed out on a lot of joys but I have no regrets. I knew what I wanted and worked hard to get it.

. . . and After

WHEN I closed the door on *The Street* for the last time, the world opened up for me. I did not do very much immediately, apart from being interviewed by Terry Wogan. It was a very entertaining evening at Shepherd's Bush where Terry made everything as pleasant and easy as it could possibly be. After that there was a lull which enabled me to have a thorough rest and a change of scene. I visited friends all over the country, friends I had not seen for ages – years in some cases – because of the total demands on my time *The Street* had made; it was almost as if I had rejoined a world from which I had taken leave over twenty years before. I went up to Ambleside to stay with Ken and Cynthia. My brother had retired in 1984 and he and Cynthia are now living in a lovely part of the Lake District where he is much involved in musical activities, composing music and accompanying other musicians.

What I appreciated more than anything was not having to get up at ten minutes to seven every morning to catch that wretched train. Never before in my life had I enjoyed the luxury of doing nothing, pleasing myself and working to my own timetable. The world outside kept on at me though and I was brought down to earth by the piles of letters I had to answer. Also I received a lot of scripts from Joan: plays, which I didn't want to do, and television scripts all with characters very similar to Hilda – little, down-trodden ladies, widows or worried housewives, women with a lot to cope with; but if I only had parts like that to consider I might as well have stayed in *The Street*. I was also asked to be in a pantomime and I didn't even bother to ask what the part was . . . probably the wicked witch . . .

Then, to my delight, came a script with a role for me which was totally different from anything I had done. It was for one of the *Boon* series and the part I was offered was that of a nosy, elderly journalist investigating the suspect owner of a gourmet hotel. It took place during a 'Who-dun-it?' holiday weekend and looked to be a good, fun part. So it turned out to be, and was made all the more enjoyable by working with people I had known before; David Daker, who had been in *The Street* as a temporary manager of the *Rovers Return*, and Michael Elphick, who I knew from his frequent visits to Granada in Manchester.

Life was busy for me once again. I was able to get in a cruise to the West Indies on the *Canberra* and a tour of Scotland with Ken, Cynthia and Joyce. After all that I was ready to work again. I have always loved the television programme *Last of the Summer Wine*, so it was a special pleasure to be asked to take part in the Christmas edition. My part was another departure from the Hilda image, being that of Auntie Wainwright who kept a second-hand junk shop in the village; an independent and determined old lady who gave Compo, Clegg and Seymour quite a hard time. I had to go to Huddersfield to do some filming in the nearby moorland village of Marsden where it was bitterly cold, but I loved doing it. The interior scenes were done in London in December. I had a reunion with Kathy Staff who had been in *The Street* some years before.

In between the two television shows I took part in *Scandal*, a film about the Profumo affair in which I played Christine Keeler's mother. It was a tiny part and only involved two days filming. I took the job because I was rather interested in comparing filming for the two media – cinema and television. In the event they proved to be very similar but my curiosity was satisfied.

What came next was totally different. I was asked to do some poetry readings for BBC 1's *Five to Eleven* series, shown each morning for a week. They were transmitted in April, 1989; among my choice of readings were: a couple of Marriott Edgar's Lancashire monologues, *The Battle of Hastings* and *The Magna Charter*, T S Eliot's *The Naming of Cats*, Harold Monro's *Milk for the Cat* and as a prose piece, a short extract from Kenneth Grahame's *The Wind in the Willows*, all of them great favourites of mine.

Also, by way of complete contrast, I have been a panellist in *Blankety Blank* with Les Dawson: that was a hilarious evening!

Now, as I write, I am preparing to go to Birmingham to take part in one of a new series for Central Television – mystery plays in which the audience is challenged to identify the guilty party.

I think by now it will be quite plain to everyone that not only have I not retired after leaving *Coronation Street* but fully intend to go on for quite a few years yet – as long as producers want me, and as long as I can stagger on to the set.

It does seem a long time since Seumas Stewart offered a job with the Adelphi Guild Theatre to a stage-struck young girl. There are so many people over the years that I have to thank for their help, encouragement and belief in me, but I think I must say, with the greatest sense of gratitude to that early source of inspiration – 'Thank you, Teddy Brown!'

INDEX

Photographic Acknowledgements

The majority of photographs in this book came from the author's private collection. The Publisher and author wish to thank the following for permission to reproduce material: the *Daily Star* for 'In my role as mascot for a Welsh Rugby team'; the *Daily Telegraph* for 'Being presented to the Queen, Palace Theatre, Manchester, 1977'; Granada Television Centre for 'With Bunny at our special anniversary party to celebrate 10 years on The Street', 'Hilda with 'Our Hilda' rose', 'With Sir John Betjeman', 'A Studio portrait, 1982', 'My leaving party with the cast of *Coronation Street*, 1987'; the *Sunday Mirror* for 'With my R.T.S. Award, 1985'; the *Sunday People* for 'Hilda with *Coronation Street*'s Bobby'; *TV Times* for 'In my conservatory', 'At home in Southport'.